Southern Counties
Main Line Steam

MICHAEL WELCH

Capital Transport

ISBN 978-1-85414-349-5

Published by
Capital Transport Publishing
www.capitaltransport.com

Printed by
1010 Printing International Ltd

Front cover: The late Ken Wightman was an early exponent of colour photography and took many pictures in the area south east of London, where he lived. He had a particular flair for taking really excellent pictures of steam locomotives in action. Here, 'King Arthur' Class No.30794 *Sir Ector de Maris*, hauling a multi-coloured rake of carriages, darkens the sky at Downsbridge Road overbridge, between Beckenham Junction and Shortlands, with a down Ramsgate train on 26th August 1957. This picture illustrates the very high technical standard of his work, not to mention his ability to press the shutter just at the right moment. Not many people were taking shots of comparable quality in 1957! *David Clark collection*

Back cover: The 9.30am Waterloo to Bournemouth West train, with Bulleid Pacific No.34001 *Exeter* in charge, enters Woking station on 28th July 1963, while a '2-Hal' electric unit stands on an adjacent track. *Exeter* was the first light Pacific to be completed, emerging from Brighton Works in June 1945, and ran in original condition until it was rebuilt in November 1957, one of the first locomotives to be converted. No.34001 lasted until the end of steam on the SR in July 1967. *Michael Chown*

Title Page: Guildford has always been an interesting railway centre, where the very busy main line from Waterloo to Portsmouth meets the cross-country secondary line from Reading to Redhill. Further interest was provided by the infrequent branch trains on the line to Horsham. In this picture, taken on 29th June 1964, Maunsell U Class 'Mogul' No.31800, in charge of the 5.05pm Reading to Redhill train, passes Ivatt-designed 2-6-2T No.41301 which is waiting to enter the station to form the 6.34pm train to Cranleigh. *Michael Chown*

Introduction

The purpose of this album is to present a representative selection of photographs of mainline steam on the Southern Region taken during the final ten years or so of operation. The geographical area covered by the book comprises what are generally regarded as the 'Southern Counties' of England, consequently the 'West Country' counties of Devon and Cornwall have been excluded. Volume Two covering the branch line scene is already in preparation. One of the most difficult decisions I have faced concerns whether or not certain secondary routes should be regarded as 'main lines' or 'branch lines'. For example, the status of the Somerset & Dorset line (S&D) is debatable and I have decided to include it in Volume Two on the basis that for most of the year only one main line long-distance train was routed via the S&D and even the line's local service was quite sparse.

The run-down of steam on the SR in the post-war period really got under way in 1957 when the first stage of the Hastings line dieselisation was inaugurated and a further ten years were to elapse until the total elimination of the steam locomotive in ordinary service. Apart from one or two odd workings, the complete dieselisation of the London to Hastings via Battle service occurred on 9th June 1958 and the powerful 'Schools' Class locomotives that had given the route such excellent service were largely displaced. The Kent Coast electrification was also accomplished in stages, the first phase from Gillingham to Dover Marine (later Western Docks) and Ramsgate being completed in June 1959. The last 'official' steam-hauled train from Victoria to Dover via Chatham was the 8.52pm departure on 14th June and this was hauled by L1 Class 4-4-0 No.31753 suitably decorated with a wreath on the smokebox door. The main part of the next stage of the Kent Coast electrification was the conversion of the route from Sevenoaks to Dover via Tonbridge, but phase two also included electrification of some secondary routes such as the Ashford to Ramsgate via Canterbury West line. The various lines involved were 'switched on' on a piecemeal basis and full electric working on all routes commenced on 18th June 1962. This meant that steam was virtually banished from the county of Kent except for three SECR C Class locomotives retained at Ashford works in departmental service for shunting purposes and a small pocket of steam operation at Tonbridge which continued to see workings off the Central Division from both the Redhill and Tunbridge Wells directions.

Next on the 'hit list' for the replacement of steam was the Central Division, where the main lines had been electrically worked since the 1930s, but steam still played a major role working van, goods and inter-regional passenger trains. In addition, the Oxted/Uckfield lines and various branches were still dominated by steam traction. Brighton shed, for example, had a complement of sixty-three steam engines on its books in the summer of 1957 ranging from diminutive 'Terrier' 0-6-0Ts to Bulleid 'West Country' Pacifics. The ousting of steam from the Oxted/Uckfield line workings by diesel units resulted in a reduction of steam diagrams, while the gradual introduction of Type 3 (later Class 33) diesel locomotives on a falling number of goods workings and withdrawal of some inter-regional passenger services further eroded the work available to steam. The final nail in the coffin for Brighton shed was the replacement of steam traction on the Horsham trains in May 1964 which left it with virtually no remaining work for steam, apart from the Lancing workmen's train which was booked to be diesel-hauled from 15th June 1964, when the shed was closed to steam. Ironically, the closure of Brighton shed coincided with an unexpected upsurge in through engine working from the London Midland Region (LMR), two regularly diagrammed turns being car-sleepers from Glasgow and Newcastle to Newhaven. The majority of those trains were handled by 'Black Fives' but, much to the amazement of local enthusiasts, two 'Jubilee' Class locomotives appeared during June. All steam engines visiting east Sussex were now sent to Eastbourne shed for servicing and on the evening of 26th June 1964 the shed contained a remarkable quartet of 4-6-0s, including a 'Jubilee', BR Standard No.73159 and a B1 Class that had earlier worked a van train to Lewes. But these workings proved to be almost the final flourish in the area and Redhill was the focal point of activity for the last months of steam on the Central Division. There were still regular steam duties on the Reading and Tonbridge lines but these routes were largely dieselised in January 1965. In June the 'Cuckoo Line' and Horsham to Guildford branch, both of which had retained steam diagrams, were closed and the long-forecast elimination of steam traction was achieved, Redhill shed closing from 14th June. In the autumn of 1965, however, the SR found itself short of electrically-heated rolling stock which resulted in the coaches used on the Brighton to Plymouth train being transferred to the Oxted Line, and steam staged a comeback on the Plymouth train, regular workings continuing until the end of the train heating season on 30th April 1966.

Unlike the Central Division, where steam traction simply faded from the scene over a protracted period, the end of steam on the South Western Division could not have been more clear cut and the whole world knew that Sunday 9th July 1967 would be the last day of steam on that Division and the SR generally. During the period covered by this book there were two major events that caused a marked reduction in steam operation, both ironically involving the Western Region (WR). The January 1963 boundary changes saw a large area of SR territory west of Salisbury transferred to the WR which later prompted a holocaust of former SR steam traction in the West Country. In September 1964 the WR introduced a revised, diesel-hauled service on the Waterloo to Exeter route which involved the withdrawal of the traditional through trains from London to the Devon/Cornwall holiday resorts and the end of the famous 'Atlantic Coast Express'. The final down weekday run of this train, on Friday 4th September 1964, saw Bulleid 'Merchant Navy' Pacific No.35022 *Holland America Line* in charge and this locomotive gave a sparkling performance, with a top speed of 88mph being attained west of Salisbury. There was also some excitement the following day when the 8.25am Plymouth to Waterloo was double-headed by a pair of un-rebuilt Bulleid Pacifics, Nos.34106 *Lydford* and 34079 *141 Squadron* officiating. The Bournemouth electrification was announced in September 1964 and this at last fixed a date for the cessation of steam services on what had become Great Britain's last steam-worked main line. During the ensuing years the SR management seized every opportunity to eliminate steam whenever possible and in August 1966 timetabled diesel-hauled passenger trains started to appear on the Bournemouth Line using 3TC/4TC units earmarked for the new electric service, while in January 1967 six WR Brush Type 4 Co-Co diesels were drafted in to supplement the ailing steam fleet that was retained on a minimal maintenance basis. Many of the speed restrictions in connection with engineering work were lifted during the last few months of steam operation and, despite the generally indifferent mechanical condition of many locomotives, some excellent performances were noted, recalling the glory days of steam on the Bournemouth line. An afternoon passenger train from Weymouth to Waterloo on 9th July proved to be the very last long distance SR main line working, and that was it!

I would like to thank all of the photographers who kindly trusted me with their precious and irreplaceable transparencies; production of this book would not have been possible without their assistance. In addition, Chris Evans, Dave Fakes, Graham Mallinson, Terry Phillips and Ian Wright have kindly read through the draft and suggested many improvements and corrections which have greatly enhanced the end product and I am most grateful to these gentlemen. Slides from the collection of the late R. C. Riley have been kindly provided by Rodney Lissenden, while the luggage labels are from the Les Dench collection. Design and typesetting by Lucy Frontani and Kate McKellar. I accept responsibility for any errors that have remained undetected.

Michael Welch
Burgess Hill, West Sussex
December 2010

Contents

An express from Victoria to Ramsgate passes beneath Downsbridge Road overbridge, between Beckenham Junction and Shortlands, on a bright day during the summer of 1958. Motive power is provided by 'King Arthur' Class No.30767 *Sir Valence* which was built by the North British Locomotive Co. in June 1925 and survived in traffic until June 1959. Most of the coaches forming the train appear to be of Maunsell design and with one exception they are in carmine and cream livery. This picture is one of many taken at this location by the late Ken Wightman, a prolific and gifted railway photographer, who for many years lived in a house which backed onto the line at this point, so he was ideally placed to record wonderfully evocative scenes such as that depicted here. *Ken Wightman / David Clark collection*

The down 'Kentish Belle', hauled by 'King Arthur' Class No.30795 *Sir Dinadan,* passes Downsbridge Road bridge on an overcast day in September 1958 shortly before it ceased operation. This train began life as the 'Thanet Belle' in May 1948, running between London and Ramsgate, but in 1951 BR decided that it should also serve Canterbury East in connection with the Festival of Britain celebrations and a three-coach portion was detached at Faversham. The train's name was changed to 'Kentish Belle' as a result. The Canterbury portion lasted only for a brief period and in 1952 the train reverted to the former arrangements with a departure from London Victoria at 11.35am while the return working from Ramsgate left there at 5.05pm. On Mondays to Fridays motive power was normally a Bulleid Pacific, but at weekends, when many extra services ran, almost any available engine could be seen, including L Class 4-4-0s. The 'Kentish Belle' was one of the more obscure BR named trains and it certainly had a short career, running for the last time on 14th September 1958. It should be noted that this train ran only in the summer months and the times quoted applied on Mondays to Fridays only. *Ken Wightman / David Clark collection*

Another shot of the relatively short-lived 'Kentish Belle'. There was a short, sharp climb at 1 in 100 from Beckenham Junction to just before Shortlands Junction and in this view U1 Class 'Mogul' No.31895 is seen working hard up the gradient with the down train on a dull day in 1957. In 1928 the solitary three-cylinder 2-6-4T No.A890 *River Frome* was converted to a 2-6-0 tender engine, a conversion that proved to be extremely successful with the result that Maunsell ordered a further twenty three-cylinder 'Moguls', Nos.A891 to A900 and 1901 to 1910 which were built in 1931. The three-cylinder U1 Class locomotives were slightly more powerful than their two-cylinder U Class sister engines. At the time of this photograph all of the U1s were allocated to sheds on the South Eastern Section. Following their displacement from that Section the U1 Class engines migrated to other areas and No.31895 was allocated to Feltham for a while before joining a large contingent of U1s based at Norwood Junction. It was withdrawn at the end of 1962 and spent a period stored in Hove goods yard before being removed for scrapping. *Ken Wightman / David Clark collection*

An up van train from Ramsgate headed by D1 Class 4-4-0 No.31739 has just passed Shortlands Junction on the last stage of its journey into London. This locomotive was originally constructed as a D Class engine in 1902 at Ashford works and rebuilt as D1 Class in 1927. It survived to become one of the last inside cylinder 4-4-0s active on the South Eastern Section and sometimes appeared on the 7.24am London Bridge to Ramsgate via Ashford train which was the last regular passenger duty for this type on the 'South Eastern'. One of No.31739's last public appearances was during the last day of services on the Dunton Green to Westerham branch when it powered a number of trains on the line assisted by Q1 Class No.33029. These workings may well have been No.31739's last revenue earning duties because it was withdrawn the following month, together with sister locomotive No.31489, and the class was rendered extinct. No.31739 is reported to have amassed 2,002,974 miles during its career which spanned fifty-nine years. *Ken Wightman / David Clark collection*

LONDON–CHATHAM–RAMSGATE

The South Eastern Section lines in the London area were some of the most heavily trafficked in Great Britain, especially in the summer months when additional trains were operated to the Kent coast resorts, and in this picture, taken on 23rd June 1957, an excursion train destined for one of the Kent resorts is pictured at Bromley South waiting for a down Ramsgate express to overtake or, possibly, waiting to reverse into the platform. The Ramsgate train is headed by an unknown 'King Arthur' Class 4-6-0 while D1 Class 4-4-0 No.31749 is in charge of the excursion working. The first four coaches of the express train are Set No.82 of Bulleid design, this being one of fifteen four-coach sets built in 1949 for services from London to the Kent coast. The excursion train is formed of 'Ironclad' Set No.471 which was originally constructed at Lancing works in the mid-1920s for use on the 'City Limited' between London and Brighton. By the time of this photograph its formation had been reduced but at least it was still in revenue-earning service. *Ken Wightman / David Clark collection*

BRITISH RAILWAYS — Southern Region

787/64

TO

BROMLEY STH.

Off it goes! The excursion train has been waiting patiently for the Ramsgate express to overtake and at last the crew of No.31749 have got the 'road' and can set off for the seaside, doubtless with a trainload of happy customers in tow who are looking forward to an enjoyable day out. At least the sun was shining brightly as the train left Bromley South! *Ken Wightman / David Clark collection*

Trains travelling in an easterly direction along the Victoria to Chatham line face a fair number of adverse gradients until Sole Street station (27 miles from Victoria) is reached. From Sole Street the line descends towards Rochester at a gradient of 1 in 100 and enginemen can take it relatively easy as their train drifts down the bank. In this shot, taken in August 1958, 'King Arthur' Class No.30796 *Sir Dodinas le Savage* runs downhill with an unidentified Ramsgate-bound working. This machine was built in May 1926 at Eastleigh works and survived in service until February 1962. During its career it worked on all three (what later became) divisions of the 'Southern' and in the 1920s could be seen on the Brighton line. It spent most of its time on the South Eastern Section, however, being based at Hither Green for a while until displaced by electrification in the late-1950s. During the twilight years of its career it saw service at Salisbury shed. *Ken Wightman / David Clark collection*

Photographed on 13th June 1959, the penultimate day of scheduled steam operation on the London to Ramsgate main line, SECR D1 Class 4-4-0 No.31749 is seen making a brisk start away from Newington with the 11.50am Victoria to Dover Priory train in tow. This train was booked to run fast from Victoria to Chatham but then became a much slower 'all stations' working and was advertised to arrive in Dover at 2.45pm. The section of line from just east of Rainham to Newington was extensively remodelled as part of the Kent Coast Electrification Scheme and became a four-track section which ended just beyond the platform ends at Newington, as seen here. D1 Class No.31749 was originally built as a D Class in 1903 by Vulcan Foundry and rebuilt as a D1 in 1921 by Beyer Peacock. After 58 years of service the end came for this locomotive in November 1961 when, accompanied by E1 Class No.31067, it powered a civil engineer's train from Bat and Ball sidings to Ashford whence neither ever returned. Sadly, no examples of either class survived into preservation. *R. C. Riley*

An up Kent Coast train, headed by an unidentified U1 Class 2-6-0, heads away from Sittingbourne, also on 13th June 1959. The train is passing Lowe's siding at which dog food from the adjacent factory is being loaded into vans. In the background the Sheerness branch is just discernible, trailing in on the left. Note the brand new colour light signal on the down line in the middle of the picture and the remains of the exceptionally tall lattice post signal it had replaced. *John Langford*

A view of Ramsgate engine shed yard (or motive power depot to give the shed its official title) on 14th May 1960, with a trio of unidentified Maunsell locomotives on view; the engine in the centre is believed to be N Class 'Mogul' No.31401. One of the first major developments by the newly-created Southern Railway was to rationalise the railway network in the Ramsgate area where the two pre-grouping companies had separate stations. In 1926 a new station was opened on a brand new section of line and the former pre-grouping stations were closed. In addition to building their new station, the Southern Railway also proposed to construct an engine shed, carriage cleaning depot and goods shed on adjacent land. The locomotive depot was authorised in 1926 at a cost of £55,000 and a six-road single-ended concrete structure was built. A brick-built water tower was provided on the northern side, a 65ft.-long turntable was installed plus a mechanical coaling plant, the last mentioned at a cost of £10,000. The opening of the new shed meant that several smaller sheds in the area became redundant, Margate West and Ramsgate Town closing in 1926 while Deal lasted until 1930, the year that the new motive power depot was commissioned. It was found that the water in the area was unsuitable for steam locomotives and in 1933 a 10,000 gallon water softening plant was authorised at a cost of £2,500. Many locomotive types were allocated to the shed during its lifetime including 'King Arthur' and 'Schools' class locomotives which, along with D1 Class engines were based there right from the opening. There was also a large contingent of H Class 0-4-4Ts, but very few goods engines were ever based at Ramsgate. In the 1950s Bulleid Pacifics and BR Standard classes became commonplace at the depot. The Kent Coast electrification of 1959 meant that Ramsgate lost its status as an independent shed, but it remained a servicing point for visiting locomotives until closing completely in December 1960. The main shed building, being of fairly recent construction, was converted into a maintenance depot for electric stock and remains in use at the time of writing.
R.C. Riley

In the days when the majority of travellers to the near continent went by train and ship there was one service that stood out above all of the others for quality, style and service – the famous 'Golden Arrow' . This train was formed mostly of colourful and beautifully maintained Pullman carriages that were particularly cosy and inviting for those people who were able to afford the supplementary fare charged. In the winter 1964 timetable the 'Arrow', as it was often called by railwaymen, was advertised to leave London Victoria at 10.00am and the scheduled arrival time at Paris Gare du Nord was 5.50pm. The sea crossing from Dover Marine (later Western Docks but since closed) took around one hour twenty minutes but no doubt in bad weather the passage took much longer! Motive power for the 'Golden Arrow' was provided by Stewarts Lane shed which always ensured that the locomotive selected was in tip-top condition both mechanically and externally. It would not do for the train's appearance to be spoiled by a dirty engine. In this shot an immaculate rebuilt Bulleid Pacific No.34088 *213 Squadron* negotiates the stiff 1 in 62 climb away from Victoria station on 10th September 1960. *R.C. Riley*

In the early 1950s a total of half a dozen 'Merchant Navy' Class Pacifics was based on the South Eastern Section at Stewarts Lane and Dover sheds, but towards the end of that decade only three un-rebuilt examples, Nos.35001 *Channel Packet,* 35015 *Rotterdam Lloyd* and 35028 *Clan Line* were active on the 'South Eastern'. In the spring of 1958 No.35015 was sent away to Eastleigh for rebuilding and later returned to Stewarts Lane shed, thus becoming the first, and only, rebuilt member of its class to work regularly on the South Eastern Section. When Phase One of the Kent Coast Electrification scheme was inaugurated in June 1959 all three locomotives (Nos.35001 and 35028 were still in un-rebuilt condition) were transferred away to Nine Elms shed on the South Western Section. In this illustration No.35015, in fine external condition, is seen passing beneath Downsbridge Road overbridge with a down continental express following its rebuilding at Eastleigh works. Sadly, later in its career *Rotterdam Lloyd* fell victim to a decree issued by Southern Region management that no further heavy repairs were to be undertaken on 'Merchant Navy' Class locomotives and, in February 1964, it became one of the first members of its class to be withdrawn from traffic.
Ken Wightman / David Clark collection

In the early 1950s two BR Standard 'Britannia' Class Pacifics, Nos.70004 *William Shakespeare* and 70014 *Iron Duke* were allocated to Stewarts Lane shed specifically to power the prestigious 'Golden Arrow' between London and the Kent coast. This photograph, which was taken towards the end of their stay on the SR, depicts No.70014 hauling the down train between Beckenham Junction and Shortlands on 4th April 1958. Later that year the two 'Britannias' were moved away from the Southern Region and transferred to Trafford Park shed, Manchester, from where they worked expresses from Manchester Central to London St Pancras. Alas, their external condition soon deteriorated because they were not afforded the celebrity status they had been given at Stewarts Lane. Note the extraordinary variety of liveries of the vehicles formed in the train – perhaps occasionally a coach in Western Region 'chocolate and cream' colours also found its way into the formation! *Ken Wightman / David Clark collection*

Iron Duke's sister engine at Stewarts Lane shed was No.70004 *William Shakespeare* which is seen in the same area at the head of the 'Golden Arrow' in the late 1950s. At the time of this photograph work was in progress to quadruple the line on this side of the bridge, hence the very untidy nature of the lineside. Once again, the train is composed of carriages displaying a remarkable variety of liveries. *Ken Wightman / David Clark collection*

This picture was taken by the late Ken Wightman who (as previously stated) lived in a house that backed onto the railway line between Beckenham Junction and Shortlands stations. Ken took numerous photographs at or near this location over the years but this picture, with Bulleid Pacific-hauled trains passing each other, was clearly an exceptional shot especially as one of the locomotives depicted was, as previously mentioned, one of only three Bulleid 'Merchant Navy' Class locomotives that ever worked regularly on the South Eastern Section in the late 1950s. The up train, headed by two unknown 'Battle of Britain' locomotives, is clearly identified by its unmistakable headboard while the down working, with No.35001 *Channel Packet* in charge, is a continental express bound for one of the Kent ports. This picture was taken on 30th March 1959, obviously the photographer's lucky day, and No.35001's career on the 'South Eastern' was not destined to last much longer for reasons stated in a previous caption. Note that the 'Battle of Britain' engines have two different types of tender. *Ken Wightman / David Clark collection*

The front coach is shrouded in steam as nicely cleaned Maunsell N1 Class 2-6-0 No.31876 gets away from Tonbridge with (what appears to be) a train to Brighton on 17th August 1957. The N1s were a three-cylinder development of the N Class and it was found that the N1s consumed less coal, but more water than their N Class sister engines and were probably more expensive to maintain so there was really little to choose between the two classes. Only six N1 Class engines were constructed, No.31876 emerging from Ashford works in March 1930. No.A876 (as No.31876 then was) was used by New Cross shed at one time on the 'Sunny South Express' between Willesden and Brighton and by 1939 it was based at Bricklayers Arms and spent most of the war years working goods trains on both the Central and South Eastern Sections. Later No.31876 was shedded at St Leonards for powering the heavy gypsum trains which originated at nearby Mountfield, on the Hastings line. The N1 Class became extinct when all six locomotives were withdrawn at the end of 1962. *Ken Wightman / David Clark collection*

The much-acclaimed glory and romance of the steam age are noticeably lacking in this shot of Tonbridge shed taken on the evening of 20th September 1959. The main line to Ashford is on the left of the picture, concealed by wagons. The locomotives on view (from left to right) include a Maunsell 'Mogul', a Bulleid Q1 Class 0-6-0, D1 Class 4-4-0 No.31749 and an H Class 0-4-4T. The cramped shed yard is covered with piles of locomotive ash which must have created a hazard for staff employed at the shed, but little seems to have been done to clear it all away – oh dear! The original shed at Tonbridge was a three-road single-ended building which probably dated from 1842 when railways first arrived in the town. The South Eastern Railway later carried out extensive alterations incorporating much of the original buildings and these resulted in the creation of a 'new' six-road through building built of brick with a pitched slated roof; there was also a 55ft. turntable and coal stage. It should be noted that two of the shed roads were 'dead end' roads accessed only from the eastern end of the depot and these are not visible in the picture. Various improvements were undertaken after the Second World War including the installation of a new asbestos roof with brick gables. Tonbridge was the last shed in Kent open to steam traction and continued to service steam engines until June 1964. *John Langford*

LONDON–TONBRIDGE–DOVER

An up express from Ramsgate/Dover to Charing Cross approaches Tonbridge behind Bulleid 'West Country' Class Pacific No.34021 *Dartmoor* in October 1958. The scene is dominated by the large elevated signal box, this being located adjacent to the junction with the line to Tunbridge Wells and Hastings which veers off to the right on a sharp rising gradient. The building in shadow beyond the signal box is the motive power depot. No.34021 was constructed at Brighton works in January 1946 and was rebuilt in December 1957; at the time of this photograph it was one of nine Bulleid Light Pacifics allocated to Ramsgate shed. *Dartmoor* was destined to last until the end of steam on the Southern Region and, indeed, on 9th July 1967 powered the very last steam-hauled boat train, the 11.00am Southampton Eastern Docks to Waterloo – a truly historic moment in railway history. *Ken Wightman / David Clark collection*

BRITISH TRANSPORT COMMISSION
BRITISH RAILWAYS   B.R. 21716/772

TONBRIDGE

The layout and infrastructure at the eastern end of Paddock Wood station is depicted in this illustration which was taken in June 1961. The station's elevated signal box stands out on the right of the shot while the tracks curving away sharply to the left are those to Maidstone West. There were two bay platforms at the east end of the premises, one for Maidstone trains on the left which is still used at the time of writing, while branch services to Hawkhurst departed from the bay on the right and passed underneath the signal box. Conductor rails are already laid preparatory to the commencement of electric services and work on an extension to the down platform appears to be proceeding, but there are no colour light signals in view and the station appears to be controlled solely by old-fashioned semaphore signals. One wonders how long they were destined to last! Note the jointed track, sections of bullhead rail and, almost out of sight, the new electric stock stored in sidings on the left in readiness for the big 'switch on'. *Gerald Daniels*

A sign of the times? When this picture of a platform sign on Paddock Wood station's down platform was taken on 20th June 1961 the passenger service on the delightfully rural Hawkhurst branch had just been withdrawn and BR could justly be accused of misleading the travelling public. One wonders how passengers unaware of the closure would have reacted when station staff politely informed them that they had missed the last train to Hawkhurst by a week or so! The decorative platform canopy ironwork will be noted. The photographer has also included (probably not intentionally!) part of 2-HAP electric unit No.6006 which was relatively new at the time, having been built in the late 1950s for phase one of the Kent Coast Electrification: this is berthed in the bay used by trains on the line to Maidstone West. *Gerald Daniels*

The last rites on the Hawkhurst branch. Following the withdrawal of passenger trains from 12th June 1961 a special train was run on 20th June to clear all of the remaining wagons – obviously it was considered that the amount of goods traffic on the line did not warrant keeping it open solely for freight. Here, very grimy C Class 0-6-0 No.31588 and its crew, plus local shunting staff, are seen posing at Paddock Wood after returning from Hawkhurst with a string of empty wagons. The staff have entered into the spirit of the melancholy occasion by embellishing their locomotive with foliage, but it must have been a really sobering experience to run back to Paddock Wood knowing that, apart from demolition workings, a train would never again venture along a line which had a relaxed and charming atmosphere all of its own. *Gerald Daniels*

Twenty-five R Class 0-6-0Ts were constructed between 1888 and 1898 at the South Eastern Railway's Ashford works to the design of James Stirling, thirteen of which were later rebuilt by Wainwright between 1910 and 1922 and re-classified R1. The rebuilt engines generally weighed 46tons 15cwt., had 5ft. 2in. driving wheels and a tractive effort of 18,480lb, but it should be noted that some locomotives had smaller wheels and a slightly higher tractive effort. No.31337, seen here at Ashford shed in April 1958, was originally built way back in June 1888 and was one of only two representatives of this little-photographed class to survive into 1960, and became the penultimate survivor. No.31047 was the last of all, being withdrawn in March of that year. This class is probably best associated with haulage/banking of heavy boat trains up the incline from Folkestone Harbour to Folkestone Junction, while some members of the class were modified with cut-down boiler mountings and retained the original Stirling round cab roofs for working the Canterbury to Whitstable Harbour line. The last-mentioned engines were 7cwt. lighter than their sister locomotives.
Derek Penney

BRITISH TRANSPORT COMMISSION
BRITISH RAILWAYS   B.R. 21716/28

ASHFORD   KENT

Folkestone Junction as you may never have seen it before! This fascinating picture was taken from the cab of D1 Class 4-4-0 No.31489 on 14th May 1960 and gives an excellent view of the track layout at this important junction, where boat trains to and from Folkestone Harbour reversed in the sidings on the right. There are no fewer than three other engines in view – one wonders what they were all doing! There was a small three-road, single-ended locomotive shed on the other side of No.31489 and in bygone times its allocation consisted mainly of R1 Class 0-6-0Ts employed on working boat trains to and from Folkestone Harbour. These locomotives were later replaced by GWR pannier tank engines. For many years the shed at Folkestone Junction was a sub-shed of Dover and it closed upon electrification in 1961. The tunnel in the background is Martello tunnel, one of three through the cliffs between Folkestone and the erstwhile Dover Marine station.
R.C. Riley

The distinctive smoke-blackened, tunnel-like entrance portal to the station, the harbour breakwaters and crane on the quayside are instant clues to the location of this picture. It is, of course, Dover Marine and this shot was taken on 4th April 1959, by which time conductor rails had already been laid in readiness for the forthcoming electrification. The locomotive undertaking a spot of shunting on the quay is a real 'old timer', O1 Class 0-6-0 No.31434, which was originally constructed as an O Class by Sharp Stewart & Co. in 1897. It was later rebuilt by Wainwright and re-classified O1. Fifty-five of these machines came into BR stock but only four examples survived into the 1960s, the final survivor being No.31065 which lasted until June 1961 and was lucky enough to be subsequently preserved. These engines looked particularly archaic because they had outside-framed tenders and their survival was no doubt due to the fact that they could be used on lightly-laid tracks barred to heavier locomotives. *R.C. Riley*

One wonders whether BR extolled the considerable advantages of working at Kearsney Loop Junction signal box when advertising vacancies for signalmen at that location. 'Panoramic views across the surrounding countryside, little rattling and vibration caused by passing trains, ample time for sunbathing between trains and few points levers to pull following closure of the loop line to Canterbury'. The local signal engineer's office must have been absolutely inundated with offers from eager applicants . There is no doubt that the signal box at this location was one of the most superbly situated of any on the SR network, the only apparent disadvantage being that the signalman had to climb a lot of stairs to reach it! The train appears to be a Ramsgate to Charing Cross working and the motive power is an extremely dirty Bulleid 'Battle of Britain' Pacific No.34078 *222 Squadron;* clearly engine cleaners were in short supply at Ramsgate shed, the engine's home depot at that time. The disused tracks on the left are those of the line to Canterbury East which were opened in July 1882 by the London Chatham and Dover Railway so it could compete with the South Eastern Railway for the traffic to Deal. In later years the line saw little use, but proved invaluable during the two world wars and also in 1953 when there were floods on the north Kent coast. The loop was later taken out of use entirely while the signal box lasted until December 1980. This picture was taken on 23rd May 1959. *R.C. Riley*

What a wonderful way to train spot! A couple of young boys sit by the side of the line captivated by the sight and sound of a Maunsell 'Schools' Class 4-4-0, thought to be No.30923 *Bradfield,* as it passes their picnic site just south of Wadhurst station in June 1957 with a train bound for Hastings. A lady, presumably their mother, stands by the foot crossing. She had obviously decided that a pleasant picnic by the lineside on a warm summer's day would be safe enough provided the boys did not stray too close to the tracks. One dreads to think how the authorities would react to such an innocent scene today, even on an un-electrified line. A photographic souvenir from another, more relaxed, period when people took more responsibility for their own safety and were probably the better for it. *Ken Wightman / David Clark collection*

7 1 11 0 6 8 2

BRITISH RAILWAYS (S)

This ticket is issued subject to the Bye-laws, Regulations and Conditions contained in the Publications and Notices of and applicable to the Railway Executive.

PLATFORM TICKET 1d.

Available ONE HOUR on DAY of ISSUE ONLY
Not valid in Trains. Not Transferable

WADHURST

TO BE GIVEN UP WHEN LEAVING PLATFORM

1 | 2 | 3 | 4 | 5 | 6

3886

Another scene at Wadhurst in June 1957, this time showing 'Schools' Class No.30937 *Epsom* hauling a train bound for Hastings. Railway historians are generally agreed that the 'Schools' Class was Maunsell's finest design and ranks as one of the most successful 4-4-0s ever to run in Great Britain. The Traffic Manager had stipulated for Hastings line duties a locomotive that would be capable of hauling a 400-ton load at an average speed of 55mph, a very tall order bearing in mind the severe loading gauge restrictions on the route, not to mention the fact that the line was very steeply graded with long climbs in each direction up to Wadhurst tunnel. In many respects the 'Schools' Class engines were a scaled down version of the 'Lord Nelsons', using the same diameter coupled wheels, outside cylinders and even the same bogie with its 3ft. 1in. diameter wheels. The first of the class appeared on the line in mid-1931 and were an instant, trouble-free success, without the frustrations encountered by Maunsell when his 'Lord Nelson' Class locomotives entered traffic. The name 'Schools' stems from the fact that the Southern Railway handled a large amount of schools traffic and their publicity department had cleverly decided to name some of the 4-4-0s after a number of the public schools they served. *Ken Wightman / David Clark collection*

A very clean L1 Class 4-4-0 No.31786, hauling a three-coach SECR 'Birdcage' set of coaches, ambles down the Hastings Line near Wadhurst station in June 1957 with (what appears to be) a local stopping train. At that time some trains advertised to call at 'all stations' south of Tunbridge Wells were through workings from London, sometimes complete with refreshment cars, while others commenced their journeys at either Tonbridge or Tunbridge Wells – this train was presumably one of the latter. Note the cattle wagon on the rear. No.31786 was constructed by the North British Locomotive Co. in Glasgow, entering traffic in April 1926; it remained in service until February 1962. *Ken Wightman / David Clark collection*

Few branch lines had the irresistible charm of the Kent & East Sussex Railway (K&ESR) which originally ran from Robertsbridge to Headcorn via Tenterden. When the passenger service was withdrawn in 1954 the section beyond Tenterden was closed completely, but the remaining part of the line remained open for goods traffic. On 12th April 1958 the Branch Line Society ran a rail tour over the route which employed two London Brighton & South Coast Railway (LB&SCR) A1X Class 0-6-0Ts and the pair is seen here at Robertsbridge being prepared for the trip. The locomotives are (from left to right) Nos.32678 and 32636. The fireman of No.32636, who controlled the water supply using the large wheels on the top of the water crane, is perched on top of the side tank while the engine takes on water and the driver chats to two gentlemen who are presumably members of BR staff. At the time of this picture both of these diminutive locomotives were allocated to St Leonards shed for powering trains over the lightly laid K&ESR, a duty that was later taken over by a diesel shunter. The remaining part of the branch was closed in June 1961. *Derek Penney*

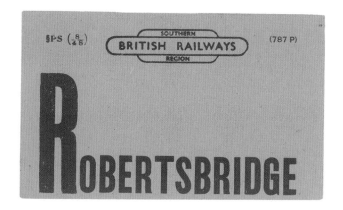

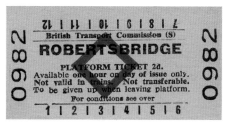

Another photograph taken in the delightful setting of Robertsbridge station. In this portrait two beautifully prepared South Eastern & Chatham Railway locomotives, H Class 0-4-4T No.31308 and D1 Class 4-4-0 No.31749, shunt the Locomotive Club of Great Britain (LCGB) 'South Eastern Limited' special train onto the K&ESR line on 11th June 1961. This train was run to commemorate the closure of the Hawkhurst and K&ESR branches and virtual elimination of steam traction from the county of Kent. The D1 Class engine depicted here certainly had a very busy day, first of all piloting L1 Class No.31786 on the initial leg of the rail tour from Victoria to Paddock Wood via Maidstone West. On arrival at Paddock Wood the participants were treated to a final trip along the Hawkhurst branch and No.31749 journeyed to Tonbridge shed for servicing. It then took the special, in double harness with the H Class locomotive, down the Hastings line as far as Robertsbridge where two A1X Class 'Terriers' took over for the run along the K&ESR to Tenterden. In the meantime No.31749 presumably went down to St Leonards to be turned, coaled and watered before returning to Robertsbridge to take the rail tour back to London, once again partnered by No.31786. What a wonderful day out for the Club's members and, doubtless, one that they wish could be repeated. Alas! *John Beckett*

When Brighton shed closed in June 1964, Redhill shed became the principal servicing point for steam traction on the Central Division and remained open for a further year, not closing until 14th June 1965 when steam was officially eliminated from the Division. Redhill shed was built by the South Eastern Railway in about 1855 and the shed's duties were mainly concerned with services on the cross-country Reading–Redhill–Tonbridge line. In 1924 the Southern Railway approved plans to rebuild the shed, but in the event only a new 65ft. turntable and modern coal stage were actually installed. BR undertook some improvements in 1950 when they provided a new standard asbestos roof. In its closing years the shed was notable for the variety of visitors from other regions, most remarkably an Eastern Region B1 Class 4-6-0 which spent a long period under repair in the autumn of 1964, while Stanier Class 5MTs became regular visitors together with Western Region 'Manor' Class 4-6-0s on an early morning train from Reading. In early 1965 the shed lost much of its importance when passenger trains on the Reading to Tonbridge route were dieselised, leaving only a small number of van trains to be worked by steam locomotives. During its last week of operation Redhill shed played host to a Class 5MT and Class 8F from the London Midland Region, both having brought down pigeon specials. On 14th June it is recorded that the shed was quite full as a result of both Eastbourne and Tunbridge Wells sheds despatching their remaining steam complement to Redhill following the closure of the 'Cuckoo' line. These engines were moved across to Guildford a few at a time and by 19th June 1965 BR Standard Class 4MT 2-6-4T No.80151 was the sole survivor; this finally departed on 26th June when the curtain came down on more than a hundred years of steam traction at Redhill. This view of the shed was taken on 10th May 1964 looking northwards. *Colour-Rail*

Opposite: In this really vintage colour view a hop pickers' special is seen at Bough Beech, between Edenbridge and Penshurst, some time in 1955. Motive power is provided by D1 Class 4-4-0 No.31494, a locomotive originally constructed as a D Class by Dubs & Co. in Glasgow in April 1903 and subsequently rebuilt as a D1 Class in the 1920s. In the 1950s hop pickers' specials were a regular sight in Kent during the autumn-time and conveyed working class families and visiting friends from the deprived, smoky inner London suburbs to the invigorating fresh air of the Kent countryside for a paid 'holiday' gathering the harvest. Increasing mechanisation reduced the demand for hop pickers and it is recorded that the last such train ran on the Hawkhurst branch in 1959, by which time these special trains had regrettably almost become a thing of the past.
Ken Wightman / David Clark collection

On the 7th October 1962 a rail tour ran down the Brighton line and, to add to the excitement of the railway enthusiast fraternity, a steam-hauled ramblers' special operated from Victoria to Nutfield, Godstone and Edenbridge. At one time there was a regular programme of such trains, which gave people who lived in the capital a rare chance to get out into the countryside and breathe some fresh air. Presumably though, if the weather was inclement, most of the participants spent as much time as possible in a local hostelry! The photographer was obviously aware that steam traction was booked to work the ramblers' train and in this picture the train is depicted near Nutfield with Bulleid 'West Country' Pacific No.34100 *Appledore* in command. An attempt had clearly been made to spruce up the locomotive for this trip, but it does not seem to be as clean as in former days during its exploits on the 'Golden Arrow'. *Ken Wightman / David Clark collection*

Burnished buffers, a newly repainted red buffer beam and the locomotive number and shed code picked out in freshly applied white paint, not to mention the rest of the locomotive absolutely polished to perfection. Brighton shed had for years enjoyed a justifiable reputation for keeping nearly all of its engines in clean condition but the manner in which they turned out *Beachy Head* for its last passenger run was simply outstanding even by their impeccable standards. In this picture No.32424 is seen at Star Lane, on the Quarry line between Coulsdon and Earlswood, hauling the Railway Correspondence & Travel Society's 'Brighton Atlantic Farewell' rail tour on 13th April 1958 which was *en route* from London to Newhaven. The Brighton 'Atlantics' were especially associated with the Victoria to Newhaven boat workings so the choice of route was apt. *Beachy Head* was the last survivor of a class of six locomotives built at Brighton works in 1911/12 and by the time of this commemorative run it had become the last engine in BR service with the 'Atlantic' (4-4-2) wheel arrangement. It spent its last years ekeing out a precarious existence mainly on the Brighton to Bournemouth through train, but also spent considerable periods in store. Tragically, on 24th April 1958, just eleven days after this iconic locomotive sped down the Brighton line, it worked an empty stock train from Lancing works to Micheldever and retired to Eastleigh shed to have its fire dropped for the last time. It was broken-up at Eastleigh works with almost indecent haste just before the preservation movement gathered force. What a sad loss! *R.C. Riley*

Opposite: The 19th March 1967 was a really sad day for 'Southern' steam fans when a Southern Counties Touring Society rail tour ran from Victoria to Brighton before continuing to Eastbourne. The train returned directly from Eastbourne to Victoria. This proved to be the last steam-hauled passenger train down the Brighton line in the BR steam era and it was unfortunate that the rostered locomotive failed at Nine Elms shed the previous evening and a very dirty substitute engine had to be provided almost at the last minute, thus marring the trip for participants and lineside photographers alike. Here, Bulleid 'West Country' Class No.34108 *Wincanton* is depicted against the unmistakable background of the erstwhile BOAC building whilst backing down into Victoria station, prior to working to Brighton. Note the turntable and coaling stage on the extreme left of the shot, but perhaps it should be mentioned that by the date of this picture steam traction had long been banished from Victoria, apart from the occasional special train. The large brick-built building in the middle of the picture is the former signal box which controlled the Central side (also known as the Brighton side) of Victoria station. *John Beckett*

The author well remembers (what were to spotters of the time) the halcyon days of steam on the Brighton line, and especially weekends in the summer when an assortment of day excursion trains often brought 'foreign' motive power to the line and provided a break from more routine goods and van train workings hauled by SR engines. In this photograph, thought to have been taken in 1962, an excursion from the London Midland Region (LMR) headed by Stanier Class 5MT No.45292 runs parallel with a Victoria to Bognor Regis train just south of Salfords station which is just visible in the background. Rather strangely the Class 5MT is hauling a rake of mostly Gresley-designed coaches that the LMR had presumably borrowed from the Eastern Region for the day. In the far distance the heavily wooded North Downs form an attractive backdrop.
Ken Wightman / David Clark collection

A most interesting picture showing a 'Hampshire' diesel-electric multiple unit, hauled by Maunsell N Class 'Mogul' No.31864, sitting in a down siding at Haywards Heath on 11th May 1963. Unfortunately, nothing is known about the circumstances of this most unusual working but presumably the unit was defective and *en route* to St Leonards depot for attention. The fact that the unit is marshalled between two brake vans indicates that it was running as an unbraked load due to the locomotive's vacuum brake being incompatible with the unit's air brake system. It is obvious from the picture that it was not *ex*-works and in any case units released from Eastleigh works were normally fit to travel under their own power to St Leonards via Havant. A real mystery photograph! *Michael Chown*

Taken from a low angle, this photograph reveals few clues regarding the location and, furthermore, nearly all of the railway infrastructure seen here has long since disappeared, apart from the two main line tracks. This picture was actually taken immediately south of Hassocks station and shows Maunsell 'Schools' Class 4-4-0 No.30925 *Cheltenham* hurrying southwards in charge of the Railway Correspondence & Travel Society's (RCTS) 'Sussex Special' rail tour on 7th October 1962. The choice of *Cheltenham* as motive power was highly appropriate because the society was founded by a group of enthusiasts in Cheltenham in 1928 and a drawing of that locomotive had been used on the cover of 'The Railway Observer', the society's monthly journal, for many years. When the Curator of Historical Relics came to select a 'Schools' Class engine for preservation it is hardly surprising that the choice fell upon No.30925 and doubtless the RCTS had at least some influence upon the decision. Later the participants journeyed along the Seaford branch with A1X Class 0-6-0T No.32636 piloting E6 Class 0-6-2T No.32418 and later travelled from Brighton to London Bridge via Steyning behind K Class 2-6-0 No.32353. *Ken Wightman / David Clark collection*

A returning Northampton to Brighton excursion, the outward working of which is seen at Salfords in a previous picture, has just left Clayton tunnel and heads towards Hassocks station. Unfortunately, the date of this shot is unknown, but it is thought to have been taken in 1962 when No.45292 was allocated to Bletchley shed. Let us hope that the good citizens of Northampton had an enjoyable outing to the South Coast! Most excursions from the LMR to Brighton around this period were powered by 'Black Fives' but one particular day, 21st May 1961, will always be remembered by local enthusiasts. That was the day when an excursion from Leicester unexpectedly produced, not a 'Black Five' as booked, but Stanier 'Jubilee' 4-6-0 No.45650 *Blake,* making the first visit of a member of its class to Brighton since 1953! The class was, apparently, officially prohibited from the Brighton line but this stipulation had clearly escaped the notice of the shed foreman at Leicester, or maybe it was a case of the locomotive being rostered in error or sent out as a late substitute for the booked engine which had failed. Whatever the reason, No.45650 was impounded by the local civil engineer and its train returned behind a 'Schools' Class locomotive. *Blake* was sent back to its home territory a fortnight later.
Ken Wightman / David Clark collection

The unmistakable outline of Brighton station's distinctive roof gives an immediate clue to the location of this picture which was taken at Brighton shed on a rather gloomy 23rd June 1956. The locomotive is one of the six LB&SCR Atlantics, No.32421 *South Foreland,* and this particular engine was built at Brighton works way back in June 1911 and was the first of its class to be completed. By the date of this picture No.32421 had fallen on hard times as little regular work remained for the class and it is possible that it had already been laid aside, being officially withdrawn from service in August 1956. Sadly, it was broken-up for scrap before the end of the year. *R. C. Riley*

In the early 1960s Brighton shed boasted a fair allocation which included Bulleid Pacifics, 'Schools' Class 4-4-0s, a selection of vintage LBSCR designs and a large complement of BR Standard tank engines, but despite this variety of classes photographers of the day always seemed to be drawn to the South Western Division which offered a multitude of steam-hauled express passenger workings and, as a consequence, steam around Brighton was little photographed in colour. One of the few pictures submitted for inclusion in this album is this pleasant shot of 'Schools' Class No.30917 *Ardingly* posing at the top of the shed yard in the soft evening sunshine in June 1962. Alas, No.30917 was not destined to remain in traffic for much longer because six months later it fell victim to the holocaust of steam traction that occurred at the end of the year. The huge building in the background is the former Brighton works where many famous and much-loved classes were constructed, including the bulk of the Bulleid Pacifics. *Alan Reeve*

People rave about the splendid view of Central station from the castle keep at Newcastle and the wonderful spectacle of a steam train climbing up to Shap summit but in the early 1960s the author's favourite view was undoubtedly that of Brighton shed seen from the top of the chalk hill that adjoins the west side of Brighton station. What a magnificent panorama of the shed and its railway environs including the impressive London Road viaduct, that carries the Eastbourne line, and the goods yard north of the station. The first shed on this site was built in 1861 and consisted of fourteen roads each with a separate arched entrance under a slated roof of several pitches. A large water softening plant was installed and a hoist provided in the middle of the shed yard. The premises were very cramped and there was no room for expansion, this situation continuing until the Brighton line electrification in the 1930s reduced the shed's importance but, even so, much work remained for steam motive power. The shed was partially reconstructed in 1938 when the slate roof was replaced by asbestos sheeting and the arches were removed. The shed closed in June 1964 after years of decline and was subsequently demolished in 1966 to make way for an engineering depot. This picture of the shed was taken on 14th September 1958 when it was still a bustling depot. *Colour-Rail*

Two 'Brighton' locomotives, A1X Class No.32636 and E6 Class No.32418, take the RCTS 'Sussex Special' rail tour up the stiff 1 in 101 gradient through Falmer station on 7th October 1962. The line climbs all of the way from Brighton station to a summit just beyond Falmer and it is likely that after almost four miles of continuous climbing with a substantial load the engine crews were pleased to see the end of the gradient coming into sight. The participants were heading for Seaford and later in the proceedings the train halted for a while at Newhaven while the locomotives were serviced on the shed. There seems to have been a very relaxed atmosphere and rail tour patrons were able to wander around the shed in glorious afternoon sunshine and photograph the two rail tour locomotives, also E4 Class No.32479 plus another 'Terrier', No.32670, which were also present. The special then returned to Brighton and made its way slowly back to the capital via Steyning. *Alan Chandler*

Preserved Drummond T9 Class 4-4-0 No.120 rounds the tight curve just beyond Lewes station with the LCGB's 'Sussex Coast Limited' rail tour on 24th June 1962. The veteran T9 Class engine apparently had a busy day, working the Waterloo to Horsham via Guildford leg of the trip before a pair of 'Brighton' tank engines took over for the run down the Mid-Sussex line to Pulborough from where the train proceeded to Midhurst. Bognor Regis was later reached behind a Billinton K Class 'Mogul' and the same locomotive took the participants to Haywards Heath where No.120 re-appeared for the trip down to Eastbourne. The T9 must have retired to Eastbourne shed for servicing and turning because it later hauled the train back to London Bridge via the outstanding and extremely heavily graded 'Cuckoo Line'; M7 Class No.30055 assisted over the most demanding section as far as Rotherfield. Full marks to the LCGB for devising a most ingenious itinerary and one that cannot be repeated!
Ken Wightman / David Clark collection

The line-up at Eastbourne shed, or at least what was left of it! Needless to say, it was a Sunday, in this case 24th June 1962, the same day that the 'Sussex Coast Limited' rail tour operated, hence there are one or two enthusiasts just discernible in the background. The BR Standard Class 4MT 2-6-4Ts, which form the bulk of the locomotives visible in this portrait, were destined to remain active in this area for a further three years, but the two Billinton K Class 'Moguls' were in their last months of service, the class being withdrawn *en masse* at the end of the year. *Gerald Daniels*

Yes, it is T9 Class No.120 again! In this picture No.120 is seen leaving Eastbourne on the final leg of the LCGB's 'Sussex Coast Limited' rail tour on 24th June 1962. The graceful T9, as previously mentioned, had a very busy day and had already performed on two different sections of this tour before embarking on what must have been by far the most strenuous part of the trip – taking the train over the very steeply graded 'Cuckoo Line' from Polegate to Eridge. The SR operating authorities were obviously taking no chances and rostered M7 Class 0-4-4T No.30055, as previously mentioned, to assist the veteran T9 over the most demanding section of the route. The M7 was detached at Rotherfield and, presumably, returned 'light engine' to Eastbourne. *Les Dench*

The East Coast line from Brighton to Hastings certainly has some fine stations and it is to be regretted that their number has been reduced by the demolition some years ago of Hastings station due to structural problems. Thankfully, the lovely station building at Eastbourne, with its splendid clock tower and lantern, is still very much in business and is seen here in this portrait which is thought to date from the early 1960s. The first station in the town was opened on a different site in 1849 and the station building seen here was designed by F.D. Bannister, and opened in 1886. Note the attractive hanging flower baskets and somewhat dated 'Southern Electric' sign – clearly the management of the day were not as image conscious as their successors. Sadly Eastbourne station was the site of a serious accident when, on 25th August 1958, the 7.45pm (previous day) Glasgow to Eastbourne sleeping car train, hauled by BR Standard Class 5MT 4-6-0 No.73042, collided with the 6.47am Ore to London Bridge service as the latter was pulling out of the station. Regrettably, five passengers aboard the electric train, which largely comprised wooden-bodied rolling stock, lost their lives while a further twenty-two passengers were injured. The crash was attributed to the excessive speed of the incoming train which allegedly passed a signal at danger. *The late K. Bannister / Stuart Ackley collection*

BRIGHTON TO EASTBOURNE

Few rail tours have had such a complicated itinerary as the LCGB's 'Wealdsman' which ran on 13th June 1965. During the course of a day it managed to include almost every route in Sussex that had either already been sanctioned for closure by the Ministry of Transport or was considered by enthusiasts to be vulnerable to closure under the Beeching Plan. Two lines, the highly scenic and fiercely graded 'Cuckoo Line' and the sleepy branch line that connected Horsham and Guildford, actually closed to passengers from the following day and the tour was the very last train over the latter which did not have a Sunday service. Needless to say local people turned out in force to witness the tour's passage over the 'Cuckoo Line', but only a few villagers took any interest in the proceedings on the Horsham to Guildford line. The tour included the Steyning line that was threatened with closure at that time and was subsequently shut down nine months later. A couple of Maunsell 'Moguls', N Class No.31411 and U Class No.31803, provided the motive power for much of the day, working from Three Bridges to Haywards Heath via Heathfield, Hastings and Eastbourne. The pair took the train over the Stonecross spur and later worked tender-first from Hastings to Eastbourne, where a turnover engine was provided to enable them to take water at what remained of the shed. This rail tour also offered patrons the rare chance of steam haulage over the Lewes to Wivelsfield line, and here the pair of Maunsell locomotives are seen passing Ditchling Common, just south of Wivelsfield where they joined the main Brighton line. In addition to commemorating the closure of the two branch lines mentioned, this train also marked the virtual end of steam traction on the Central Division of the Southern Region, so it was quite a melancholy occasion. *John Beckett*

A Brighton to Horsham train, headed by Ivatt Class 2MT 2-6-2T No.41313, rolls into Hove station on 3rd May 1964, the last day of steam on these trains. Services to Horsham were usually formed of three coaches, but on this occasion a complement of six carriages was provided, perhaps to cater for enthusiasts and local people who wished to have a final steam-hauled ride over the line before diesel units took over the following day. Six coaches constitute a heavy load for one of these moderately powered tank locomotives – let us hope it was in good 'nick'. The cessation of steam working on the Brighton to Horsham line was the final nail in the coffin for Brighton shed which, as previously stated, closed its doors six weeks later. No.41313, a Crewe product dating from May 1952, was subsequently preserved and was a resident of the Buckinghamshire Railway Centre for many years but, at the time of writing, is at Haven Street on the Isle of Wight. *Les Dench*

The 10.25am Brighton to Plymouth train, hauled by BR Standard Class 5MT No.73155, is seen passing Shoreham Airport in March 1966. The re-appearance of steam traction on this service, eighteen months after the closure of Brighton shed, was due to the fact that the SR was desperately short of electrically heated loco-hauled stock and the set allocated to this service had to be transferred to the Oxted Line at short notice in November 1965. A steam-heated set was provided for the Brighton to Plymouth train and at first Southern Railway-designed electric locomotives (known to enthusiasts as 'Hornbies') were used to power this train as far as Chichester, where steam took over, but they soon developed train heating boiler problems and steam traction started to be used from Brighton. It is recorded that the locomotives came across from Fratton to Hove, where the stock was stabled, very early in the morning to pre-heat the carriages. This arrangement lasted until the heating season ended at the end of April. No fewer than forty different engines, mostly Bulleid Pacifics, were noted on this working during that time. Shoreham Airport Halt, located near to this spot, is believed to have been the first airport station in Great Britain. It was originally opened as Bungalow Town Halt on 1st October 1910 to serve a number of rather basic dwellings that had sprung up on the west side of the river Adur. It was closed on 1st January 1933 but was reopened as Shoreham Airport Halt on 1st July 1935, only to be closed again permanently on 15th July 1940 as a wartime security measure. *Ian Wright*

Worthing Central station's most interesting working of the day! The 10.25am Brighton to Plymouth train, hauled by No.73093 which is leaking steam from every pore, eases (wheezes?) away from its Worthing stop in March 1966. The train in the other platform is a '2-Bil' electric unit marshalled at the rear of a train forming a local service. These units, which dated from the mid-1930s, were destined to remain in traffic for a further five years from the time of this picture. The three gables in the middle of the photograph (which still survive at the time of writing) originally formed part of the second station built on this site, the long canopy beyond them being constructed when the third station was built. *Ian Wright*

Yes, it is the Brighton to Plymouth train once again, which was the only steam train (with its corresponding return working) along this section of line when this picture was taken in February 1966. The train was photographed between West Worthing and Durrington-on-Sea stations and the motive power on this occasion is very dirty BR Standard Class 5MT No.73085, formerly *Melisande*. Note that the formation appears to be made up of a 'scratch' set of coaches and includes BR Standard carriages in both green and maroon liveries and one Bulleid vehicle. The large West Worthing carriage berthing shed, which has since been razed to the ground, can just be discerned in the distance. *Ian Wright*

In the late 1950s when Brighton shed had a quintet of Bulleid Pacifics for use on the through train to Bournemouth and long distance services to Plymouth and Cardiff, it maintained its complement of five 'West Country' Class engines in sparkling condition, the author's favourite being No.34045 *Ottery St Mary*. But by the time of this photograph steam traction on the SR was on its way out and suffering a deliberate policy of 'minimum maintenance', which meant that staff were required to do only the minimum necessary to keep engines serviceable and in a safe condition. Cleaning was, therefore, very low down the priority list and in this picture an indescribably filthy Bulleid 'Battle of Britain' Class locomotive, No.34060 *25 Squadron* approaches Goring-by-Sea station with the Plymouth to Brighton through train in March 1966. The goods yard has been lifted, but the loading gauge still stands as a reminder of more prosperous times. One wonders what the former Brighton shed master would have had to say about the disgraceful condition of No.34060! *Ian Wright*

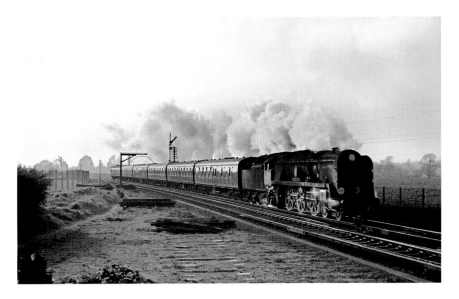

The brilliant afternoon sunshine beautifully illuminates Maunsell U Class 'Mogul' No.31791 as it leaves Havant with the empty stock of the LCGB's 'Hayling Farewell' rail tour on 3rd November 1963. The participants had transferred to another set of coaches for their nostalgic run down to Hayling Island and the main train was presumably being moved to Chichester, where it would have been stabled for a time before returning to Havant to pick up the passengers. No.31791 had earlier assisted Bulleid Pacific No.34088 *213 Squadron* for the short journey from Fratton down the Portsmouth dockyard branch and back, and then took the train to Havant without assistance, but these were its only tasks and one wonders whether it was specially cleaned for the occasion; anyway, it certainly looked nice! *Gerald Daniels*

Unfortunately, following electrification of the Horsham to Arundel Junction (Mid-Sussex line) in the 1930s, very few colour pictures of ordinary steam workings appear to have been taken on the route so the author has resorted to photographs of rail tours which, if the shots in this section are representative, always seemed to run on sunny days! The 24th June 1962 was clearly a nice, bright day and in this picture the LCGB's 'Sussex Coast Limited', hauled by a brace of 'Brighton' engines, E4 Class No.32503 piloting E6 Class No.32417, runs down the Mid-Sussex line *en route* from Horsham to Midhurst. The tank locomotives later returned to Pulborough from where K Class 'Mogul' No.32353 took over for the next section of the trip to Bognor Regis. This shot was taken just south of Christ's Hospital station, part of which is just visible in the background.
Ken Wightman / David Clark collection

A quiet autumn afternoon down by the river. The still waters of the river Arun at Pulborough reflect the trees and bushes lining the bank plus some of the bridge. Here, the LCGB's 'Midhurst Belle' rail tour, hauled by Maunsell Q Class 0-6-0 No.30530, crosses the bridge just south of Pulborough station on its way back from Midhurst on 18th October 1964. This train was the last passenger train to reach the Sussex town which, at one time, was served by three routes. After running round in the station the Q Class engine then took the passengers down to Littlehampton from where the train proceeded to Brighton behind 'Merchant Navy' Pacific No.35007 *Aberdeen Commonwealth*, which was undoubtedly quite a remarkable sight on the West Coast line. No.30530 followed No.35007 almost immediately because its services were needed to haul the participants on the next stage of the trip to and from Kemp Town. The tour ended with a high speed run up to London Victoria behind *Aberdeen Commonwealth*.
Martin Smith

The LCGB's 'Sussex Coast Limited', which is seen in previous photographs, approaches Amberley behind LBSCR K Class 'Mogul' No.32353 on 24th June 1962. This classic photographic location is enhanced by the presence of a horse and foal in the field on the right of the picture which seem to be hurrying away from the railway line – perhaps they were frightened by the steam train. Amberley castle and its adjacent church are prominent in the background on the right while on the distant horizon the thickly wooded slopes of the North Downs can just be discerned. Sadly, No.32353, which had been given a general overhaul at Eastleigh works during the previous year, had only a further six months' life remaining. It was withdrawn, together with all of the other surviving members of its class, at the end of 1962 when this distinctive and much-loved class was sacrificed for accountancy reasons, just before the British Railways Board came into being. Note that the photographer was very lucky to obtain this picture, because the electric train on the up line has only just cleared in time. *John Beckett*

One of the most attractive routes covered by this album is the line from Redhill to Reading, especially the section between Redhill and Guildford which runs parallel to the North Downs escarpment for mile after mile. It is hard to believe that some of the best scenery is around Dorking which is little more than twenty miles from the centre of London. In days gone by the line carried substantial goods traffic and some daily inter-regional trains, such as the 7.35am Birkenhead Woodside to Margate which is seen here approaching Reigate in September 1958 with BR Standard Class 4MT 2-6-0 No.76060 in charge. This train was just the kind of working that made the study of railways so rewarding in times past but also, alas, the type of working that has long since disappeared from the timetable. In the summer 1957 public timetable the train was advertised to convey a restaurant car and through coaches linking Birkenhead with Folkestone, Dover, Deal and Sandwich in addition to Margate via Canterbury West and Ramsgate. There were also through carriages from Chester to Brighton, Eastbourne and Hastings so,

in effect, it was actually three trains combined into one. One wonders how many times passengers who found themselves in a crowded part of the train decided to move to a coach that had more room only to end up at the wrong destination. It was so easily done! Travelling on the 7.35am must have been quite an experience because it was a very long journey and not advertised to reach the Kent resorts until just before 5.00pm, so it is just as well it included a restaurant car. *Roy Hobbs*

The Redhill to Reading line, as previously stated, was a main artery for goods traffic and in this shot, taken from the same location as the previous picture, a very dirty Maunsell N Class 'Mogul' No.31865 approaches Reigate with a mixed goods in tow. The line climbs at 1 in 142 against eastbound trains at this location, so the locomotive was probably working hard as it passed the photographer's vantage point. *Roy Hobbs*

Trains from the Midlands to the south coast regularly brought Western Region motive power to the Redhill to Reading line and in this picture 'Manor' Class 4-6-0 No.7813 *Freshford Manor* is seen passing the site of Buckland sidings, between Reigate and Betchworth, with such a working in June 1961. The sidings here used to serve a tile works but during the Second World War the site was converted to an ammunition and petrol storage depot and extra sidings were installed for this purpose. A loop line was provided on the up line and a signal box constructed to control movements so it must have been a quite a busy spot in its heyday. When this picture was taken, however, the site appears to have been derelict. Note that the train seems to be made up of a combination of former GWR and LMSR coaches. *Roy Hobbs*

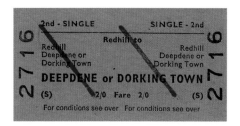

The low angle of the sun beautifully illuminates Maunsell N Class 'Mogul' No.31831 as it takes the LCGB's 'Maunsell Commemorative' rail tour up the 1 in 142 gradient east of Betchworth on 3rd January 1965. This tour was timed to coincide with the dieselisation of the Reading to Tonbridge service, which was largely the preserve of the Maunsell 'Moguls', and it was thought that the remaining twelve N Class and ten U Class locomotives might not have much longer to live following their displacement from this cross-country route. In the event these 'maids of all work' lasted much longer than most people expected and even retained some regular passenger work, such as the 4.10pm Southampton Terminus to Bournemouth, well into 1965. Their principal duties towards the end, however, were on ballast trains in connection with the Bournemouth electrification and this mundane and unglamorous work kept N Class Nos.31405/8 and U Class 31639 and 31791 occupied until they were withdrawn from Guildford shed during June 1966. *Michael Chown*

Maunsell N Class 'Mogul' No.31411 is seen at the head of an eastbound train just east of Betchworth station on 27th July 1963. This locomotive later became something of a celebrity engine because in 1965 and early 1966 it was used regularly on rail tours and made at least six appearances on enthusiasts' specials during that period before its withdrawal in April 1966. Needless to say its external appearance benefited from these assignments. The train is comprised of two Maunsell 2-sets, these being formed in 1962 when the SR operating authorities took the decision to split all of the remaining Maunsell 4-sets into two 2-coach sets – note that the brake vans are adjacent to each other in this photograph. The vans marshalled immediately behind the locomotive are a GWR fruit van (known as a Fruit D) and two horseboxes, the first being of LNER design while the other is apparently an LMSR vehicle, so this is quite an interesting train. *Alan Reeve*

In the 1960s BR pursued a relentless policy of demolishing station buildings to reduce costs, especially those that were seen as being far too large for the amount of traffic on offer. At the same time conductor guards were becoming an everyday feature of rail travel and issuing tickets on board trains was clearly an effective way of achieving substantial staff savings without greatly inconveniencing passengers. So, many stations had their buildings unceremoniously razed to the ground and were provided with basic bus stop-type shelters. The total removal of all staff meant, of course, that the days of a welcoming coal fire in the booking hall and fresh flowers on the waiting room table were well and truly over. The commodious main station building at Dorking Town station (later renamed Dorking West) was located on the westbound platform and was apparently provided with substantial living accommodation for the station master. All of this was fine in the 19th century when the station was no doubt one of the focal points of the local community but hardly suitable for BR's requirements in the second half of the 20th century, and the premises seen here were swept away as part of BR's 'scorched earth' policy. Note that, most strangely, the telegraph poles run in front of the station building and there is actually a pole in the station yard. This picture was taken on 10th May 1964. *Stuart Ackley collection*

The light is starting to fade, the shadows are lengthening and, no doubt, the temperature would have been dropping at the end of what appears to have been a perfect summer's day. In this illustration the 7.09pm from Redhill to Reading, with an unknown Maunsell 2-6-0 in charge, is seen passing Ranmore Common as it accelerates away from its Dorking Town station stop on 27th July 1963. A Bulleid-designed 3-set forms the train. In the distance the wooded slopes rise towards Leith Hill, the highest point in the southern counties. *Michael Chown*

The North Downs form a very attractive backdrop to this picture of the 11.36am Redhill to Reading train entering Gomshall & Shere station on 28th July 1963. Motive power is provided by Maunsell N Class 'Mogul' No.31823 of Redhill shed. Shortly before this picture was taken the train would have been climbing out of the river Mole valley on a long 1 in 96 gradient that presented a stern test for crews of heavy goods trains, but the climb would hardly have been noticed by No.31823 hauling a featherweight three-coach load. *Michael Chown*

Between Ash and just beyond Blackwater station the Redhill to Reading line runs through the river Blackwater valley and in this view a Redhill-bound train is seen ambling along behind Maunsell 'Schools' 4-4-0 No.30901 *Winchester* on 6th September 1962, a far cry from this locomotive's more exacting former duties on Hastings line expresses. The train has just left Farnborough North station and heads for its next station stop at, presumably, North Camp. Sadly, *Winchester* was reaching the end of its days when this shot was taken as it was one of the surviving members of the class withdrawn in the purge of steam traction at the close of the year. The bridge in the background carries the 'South Western' main line over the tracks of the cross-country route. *Derek Penney*

In this typical scene, thought to have been taken in the early 1960s, N Class No.31868 pulls away from Crowthorne with a Reading to Redhill train formed of a Maunsell 4-set. In addition to the regular through train to and from Birkenhead already mentioned there were through rush-hour workings to and from London Bridge but these trains, like the majority of the others on the line, stopped at all stations which was hardly an inducement to travel. *Ken Wightman / David Clark collection*

Unlike the rest of the route, a short section at the northern end of the Portsmouth Direct line saw regular steam-hauled passenger trains in the form of workings on the Guildford to Redhill cross-country line and branch trains on the Horsham route, which diverged at Shalford and Peasmarsh junctions respectively. Booked steam duties on the Redhill route ceased in January 1965 when diesel units took over, while steam continued on the Horsham branch until this service was withdrawn in June 1965. In this shot Ivatt-designed Class 2MT 2-6-2T No.41223 has just emerged from the tunnel immediately south of Guildford station on the first stage of its wander down the sleepy branch line to Cranleigh and Horsham. This picture was taken on 27th July 1963. No.41223 was formerly based on the London Midland Region and was a resident of Watford shed for some years before it moved to the SR in December 1962. *Alan Reeve*

When electrification work was taking place on the Bournemouth Line in the mid-1960s it was customary to undertake much of this at weekends and, to give the engineers as much freedom as possible, trains were often diverted to other routes, some of which did not normally see any scheduled steam-hauled passenger services. So, for the steam enthusiasts of the day the electrification was not entirely bad news – well, it was almost entirely bad, but not quite! On 20th March 1966 track work at Eastleigh necessitated all main line Waterloo to Bournemouth and vice versa services being diverted via Haslemere and Fareham, thus giving steam fans the rare opportunity of steam haulage over the entire length of the Portsmouth Direct line on an ordinary passenger train. Here BR Standard Class 5MT No.73114 *Etarre* shatters the peace of a quiet Sunday afternoon in the Hampshire countryside as it heads northwards up the 1 in 100 north of Rowlands Castle. This is one of the few open stretches of line on this route which is not particularly photogenic owing to the close proximity of woodland to the lineside. *Roy Hobbs*

A total of forty-five BR Standard Class 3MT 2-6-2T locomotives was constructed at Swindon works between 1952 and 1955 for light passenger work and were derived from the Great Western Railway's '6100' Class with almost identical boilers. They were mainly based on the Southern and Western regions, the last survivors being Nos.82019 and 82029 which were both allocated to Nine Elms shed for passenger duties on the Kensington (Olympia) to Clapham Junction service and empty stock workings between Waterloo and Clapham Junction. In this picture a rather anonymous looking No.82019 is seen standing in Waterloo station on pilot duties on 30th June 1967. On the penultimate day of steam on the 'Southern', 8th July 1967, it is recorded that No.82019, accompanied by BR Standard 2-6-4T No.80015, travelled to Salisbury where redundant steam engines were being congregated prior to disposal. Its sister locomotive No.82029 went out in a blaze of glory, however, at the head of the 7.18am Waterloo to Salisbury, probably its first main line passenger outing for a long time.
Roy Denison

At first sight this picture appears to depict a Union Castle boat train awaiting departure from Waterloo station, but the presence of steam enthusiasts who are leaning out of the windows indicates that it is very unlikely to be a boat train. The picture was taken on 30th June 1967, during the penultimate week of steam on the Southern Region, and actually shows the 6.54pm Waterloo to Salisbury waiting to leave with Bulleid 'Battle of Britain' Pacific No.34060 *25 Squadron* in charge. The train on the left of the photograph, which has a Western Region 'Warship' diesel-hydraulic locomotive at the head, is likely to be the 7.00pm to Exeter, while the carriage in the adjacent platform is probably part of a 4-Cor electric unit. The reason for the appearance of the rather dirty Union Castle headboard on the front of a working bound for Salisbury may never be known but it is likely that some comedian at Nine Elms shed put the headboard on No.34060, possibly to mark the retirement of a driver who was working his last trip. It certainly was not the engine's last trip because that survived into the final week of steam traction. *Roy Denison*

Steam enginemen are seen in classic pose as their train heads into the evening sun. The fireman of Bulleid Pacific No.34009 *Lyme Regis* leans out of the cab, clearly contented with the level of boiler pressure showing on the gauge, while the driver is seen in silhouette with his hand firmly gripping the regulator. This fine panned shot shows the 7.54pm Waterloo to Basingstoke train approaching Clapham Junction on 18th July 1964. *Lyme Regis* was built at Brighton and out-shopped in September 1945. It was rebuilt in January 1961 and lasted in traffic until October 1966. *Michael Chown*

A total of only five H16 Class 4-6-2Ts was built at Eastleigh to the design of R.W. Urie in 1921/22 and the class was similar in many respects to the same designer's G16 Class 4-8-0Ts, certain components being interchangeable. These engines were constructed principally for powering the transfer goods trains between the newly built Feltham hump marshalling yard and Willesden/Brent. In later years, however, they could be seen at the head of Ascot race specials and, more commonly, working empty stock trains between Waterloo and Clapham Junction. In this shot No.30519 is seen at Clapham Yard on 25th August 1957 coupled to (what appears to be) a shunter's wagon and an unidentified Maunsell-designed vehicle. No.30519 was released to traffic in January 1922 and lasted in service until the entire H16 Class was eliminated at the end of 1962.
Ken Wightman / David Clark collection

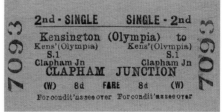

The 'Bournemouth Belle' offered the ultimate in style, luxury and opulence for passengers wishing to travel from London to Southampton or Bournemouth and in this portrait Bulleid 'Merchant Navy' Class Pacific No.35030 *Elder Dempster Lines* is seen threading Clapham cutting with this famous train in tow in September 1964. The 'Belle', as it was known colloquially to most railwaymen, first appeared in 1931 initially operating daily only in the summer period and on Sundays throughout the year. In January 1936 all-year-round daily working was introduced and invariably the train was hauled by a 'Lord Nelson' Class 4-6-0. Operation was suspended during the Second World War and when it was resumed after the end of hostilities Bulleid's 'Merchant Navy' Class Pacifics became the regular motive power. The sight of an immaculate Pacific at the head of a rake of colourful Pullman cars must have been a tonic for many people at a time of post-war food and fuel deprivations. A modest supplement was charged for travel in the beautifully appointed Pullman cars and in the 1966/67 timetable the first class supplement for travel between Waterloo and Bournemouth was 8s. 0d. (40p) while economy-minded passengers could travel in the second class accommodation for 6s. 0d. The 'Belle' was rostered for steam traction until January 1967 when Brush Type 4 diesel-electric locomotives, which had been commandeered from the Western Region to assist the ailing steam fleet, supposedly took over. In reality, however, the diesels proved to be temperamental machines and steam traction frequently came to their rescue, with Bulleid Pacifics making at least two forays on the 'Belle' during the final week of steam on the Southern Region. It had been hoped that the 'Belle' would be steam-hauled on its last day of operation, 9th July 1967, but the SR management decreed that the train must be diesel hauled to emphasise their 'modern image'. This led to accusations that they were unimaginative and out of touch. *Derek Penney*

In the early 1960s, before the impact of jet-age air travel started to be felt by the shipping companies, boat trains conveying passengers to Southampton Docks were a familiar sight on the South Western Section main line. The locomotives hauling these workings often carried distinctive headboards and in this shot bystanders are left in no doubt that this train was carrying people who had booked on a Cunard liner, possibly one of their legendary flagship vessels, the *Queen Mary* or *Queen Elizabeth*. What a wonderful journey – steam haulage from Waterloo followed by a sailing from Southampton on one of the finest vessels ever to sail the seven seas. Note that the train offers exclusively first class accommodation, the second vehicle being a first corridor carriage without the cream cantrail stripe. The coach immediately behind the locomotive is a brake composite corridor with the first class seating marshalled adjacent to the rest of the train. The operating authorities would no doubt have preferred to use a brake first corridor coach, but there were no carriages of this type based on the SR. The locomotive depicted in this September 1964 shot, 'Battle of Britain' Pacific No.34072 *257 Squadron*, was withdrawn shortly after this portrait was taken and consigned to Barry scrap yard. It was later resurrected and restored to working condition but is inactive at the time of writing. *Derek Penney*

A brilliant sky with puffy clouds scudding across, the low angle of the sun and a perfectly timed smoke effect have all combined to produce a sparkling image of 'Battle of Britain' Pacific No.34109 *Sir Trafford Leigh-Mallory* approaching Earlsfield station. What a pity the engine is in such scruffy condition. The Pacific was working the 5.00pm Waterloo to Exeter train and this picture was taken on 14th May 1964. No.34109 was destined to last in service only a further four months after this picture was taken, being withdrawn in September 1964. At first sight the photographer appears to be standing in a dangerous position, but he was a professional railwayman at the time and almost certainly had the necessary authorisation to stand close to the electrified running lines. *Gerald Daniels*

Left: Yes, it is the renowned 'Bournemouth Belle' again, and this time it is seen west of Wimbledon station in charge of 'Merchant Navy' Pacific No.35011 *General Steam Navigation* on 20th May 1964. Note that at the time of this photograph the train comprised a rake of classic Pullman cars but, regrettably, towards the end of its career the Belle's Pullman brake vehicles were replaced by BR Standard full brake vehicles, commonly known as BGs, thus robbing this celebrated train of some of its character. Note also (what appears to be) a Drewry 204hp diesel shunting locomotive on the right of the shot and, in the far distance, an electric unit approaching Wimbledon station on the up local line. In the days before the standardisation of track layouts some quite interesting track features and formations could be seen, such as the profusion of diamond crossings in this photograph. *Gerald Daniels*

Below: A down Bournemouth express roars through Woking with Bulleid 'West Country' Class No.34040 *Crewkerne* in charge. By the time of this photograph, September 1966, BR's corporate image policy was beginning to take effect and some coaches were starting to appear in blue and grey livery as evidenced here by two BR Standard carriages in the train's formation. No SR Bulleid coaches were ever repainted in the new colours, but some Bulleid carriages that had been transferred to the Western Region in the 1963 boundary changes were repainted in maroon at Swindon works, however, and must have looked really strange in that livery – at least they were not repainted in 'chocolate and cream' colours! Bulleid coaches also operated in maroon livery on both the Eastern and Scottish Regions. The first station on this site was called 'Woking Common', the settlement of that name being 1 mile distant. This station consisted at first of only one platform, but two platforms and one middle road for trains not booked to stop were soon provided. The premises underwent drastic changes in the late 1930s in readiness for electrification, being rebuilt with four through tracks, and its semaphores were replaced by colour light signals. Originally, movements in the station area were controlled by three signal boxes but these were reduced to one which was constructed in 1937 at the west end of the station. *Ian Wright*

Opposite: Has there ever been a more fascinating and attractive machine than the steam locomotive? The idea of power being produced by means of a combination of fire and water is irresistible, and in this picture a small boy, who is apparently being supervised by an adult, peers out of the window immediately behind the locomotive as Bulleid Pacific No.34001 *Exeter* takes water at Woking while powering the 9.30am Waterloo to Bournemouth West train on 28th July 1963. The young fireman stands on the back of the tender, hopefully ensuring that all of the water is going where it is intended – a platform end ritual that, alas, is no longer seen. At the time of this picture the announcement of the Bournemouth electrification scheme was more than a year away; steam traction was still the pride of the fleet and virtually unchallenged on the routes to Exeter and Weymouth, many locomotives still being maintained in pristine condition, as seen here. Those were the days! *Michael Chown*

The location of this picture is clearly displayed on the giant green-painted lineside sign. The identity of the train is uncertain but it appears to be the 7.17am SuO Yeovil Town to Waterloo, which reversed at Yeovil Junction and then stopped at most intermediate stations to Salisbury before taking on the identity of a semi-fast service; after Salisbury it called only at Andover Junction, Basingstoke, Woking and Surbiton and was booked to arrive at Waterloo at 10.38am. Motive power is Bulleid 'Battle of Britain' Pacific No.34109 *Sir Trafford Leigh-Mallory*. One wonders how many citizens of Yeovil would have wanted to travel to the capital at such an early hour on a Sunday morning! Note that the formation of the train contains some of Bulleid's earliest locomotive hauled coaches which had a door to each compartment. These were used on London to the West-of-England and Bournemouth/Weymouth services for a time but were ousted by Bulleid's later designs that were considered more suitable for long-distance services. This picture was also taken on 28th July 1963. *Michael Chown*

An interesting picture of a type of train that appears to have been rarely photographed – a civil engineer's department ballast working, or, to be more precise, in this case an empty ballast working! The location is, once again, Woking where the vast civil engineer's permanent way depot can be seen on the left of the shot. This picture shows 'West Country' Pacific No.34048 *Crediton* in charge of a train of ballast hoppers and this photograph was taken on 19th October 1965. At the time of this picture the electrification of the Bournemouth line was proceeding apace and a major part of this huge scheme was the extensive track renewals that were needed for the new high speed services, so the yard at Woking would have been a hive of round-the-clock activity. *Crediton* was one of five Bulleid Pacific locomotives that were based at Brighton for many years until it was rebuilt in March 1959. It was withdrawn from service in March 1966. *Martin Smith*

A down express from Waterloo passes Farnborough on 9th September 1962 with Bulleid 'Battle of Britain' Class Pacific No.34051 *Winston Churchill* in charge. Some years later this locomotive achieved considerable fame when it hauled Sir Winston Churchill's funeral train from Waterloo to Handborough in Oxfordshire on 30th January 1965. No.34051 was turned out in absolutely superb condition, as befitted such an occasion, and a decision was subsequently made to add this locomotive to the list of those scheduled for preservation by the Curator of Historical Relics in place of No.34002 *Salisbury* which was subsequently scrapped. No.34051 did not last much longer in service after this historic event, being withdrawn in September 1965. *Rodney Lissenden*

An immaculately clean Bulleid 'Merchant Navy' Class Pacific No.35014 *Nederland Line* is seen in full flight passing Farnborough with the down 'Atlantic Coast Express' on 6th September 1962. This multi-portioned train, which conveyed through coaches from London to some of the seaside resorts on the coasts of Devon and Cornwall, was surely one of the most famous of all the SR's named trains and it was certainly one of the most long-established. The 'Atlantic Coast Express', or 'ACE' as it was known to railway enthusiasts and staff, first ran way back in 1926 and at that time motive power was usually a 'King Arthur' Class 4-6-0, presumably hauling Maunsell stock. Operation was suspended during the Second World War but when it resumed in May 1946 the rolling stock forming the train had changed beyond recognition, with Bulleid Pacifics replacing the smaller 'King Arthur' Class locomotives while the coaching stock was generally brand-new vehicles, also of Bulleid design – what a complete transformation. By the early 1960s the timings of the 'ACE' had been speeded-up east of Exeter to the extent that it had become the tightest schedule of any train in Great Britain on which steam traction was regularly employed. For example, the 83 miles-long stretch from Waterloo to Salisbury was booked to be covered in 80min. and this with a very heavy twelve coach train. The Waterloo to Exeter service was scheduled to be taken over by Western Region 'Warship' diesel-hydraulic locomotives from the start of the winter 1964/65 timetable and the last up steam-hauled 'ACE' ran on 14th August 1964 following the introduction of a number of those machines. The final down ordinary weekday 'ACE' ran on Friday 4th September 1964 with No.35022 *Holland America Line* in command, and a sparkling performance no doubt lifted the spirits of enthusiasts on board the train despite the very sad occasion. So, one of the SR's best-known and most celebrated named trains faded into history. *Derek Penney*

Bathed in absolutely perfect evening sunshine, Bulleid 'Battle of Britain' Pacific No.34054 *Lord Beaverbrook* is seen near Cove, just west of Farnborough, in charge of an unidentified up train in October 1959. At the time of this photograph No.34054 was allocated to Salisbury, a shed noted for the high standard of cleanliness of its locomotives to which *Lord Beaverbrook* bears ample testament. Constructed at Brighton, No.34054 was released to traffic in January 1947 and lasted in service until September 1964. Many of the coaches forming the train are of Maunsell design, a type of coach that was rapidly being phased out at that time. *Derek Penney*

Not surprisingly, in view of their dominance on the line, photographs of Bulleid Pacifics form the bulk of the coverage of the Waterloo to Basingstoke section of line and beyond. But, for a change, here is something different, a picture of Maunsell S15 Class 4-6-0 No.30833 heading a long down freight near Farnborough on 12th September 1964. This picture gives a reasonable indication of the footplate conditions on a steam locomotive in ordinary service and some of the hazards that enginemen took in their stride, such as coal dust flying about and, occasionally, smoke blowing down and obscuring the view forward. The class was constructed in various batches during a seventeen-year period from 1920 to 1936, and this particular engine was built as part of one of the intermediate batches and released to traffic in November 1927. It was fitted with a six-wheeled tender for working on the Central Section. It remained in service until May 1965 and all other surviving members of the class were withdrawn during that year. Sister engine No.30837 was, however, specially retained after its official withdrawal to work two rail tours in January 1966. *Michael Chown*

In steam days the traffic density on the 'South Western' main line was not as great as it is today but, even so, it was still an extremely busy stretch of line, as exemplified here by this shot of 'Merchant Navy' Pacific No.35017 *Belgian Marine* speeding westwards in charge of an unidentified express on 12th September 1964, the same day that the previous shot was taken. Just as the photographer was about to press the camera's shutter to photograph No.35017 an unrebuilt Bulleid Pacific, laying a considerable smokescreen across the Hampshire countryside, hove into view at the head of a London-bound express. The grass-covered platforms that are just visible are those of the erstwhile Bramshot Halt which was opened for the benefit of members of the Bramshot golf club on 10th May 1913; platforms were provided only on the slow lines. During the Second World War the army established the huge Cove Camp on the golf course, but in 1942 four down and two up trains were still advertised to call there 'for club members'. The halt was closed from 6th May 1946, but eighteen years later the platforms were still very much in evidence, as seen here.
Michael Chown

Tangible signs of the upgrading of the Bournemouth line were apparent when this shot was taken at Fleet in September 1966 – the third rail is already *in situ*, the steelwork is in place for new colour light signals, the up platform is being extended and a pile of concrete troughing litters the down platform. All of this bodes ill for the air-operated lower quadrant signals that had been a distinctive and interesting feature of the Brookwood to Basingstoke section for many years, and also for 'Merchant Navy' Pacific No.35013 *Blue Funnel* hurtling through with its train of mostly Bulleid carriages. Note that the first two coaches immediately behind the engine are BR Standard Mk.1 vehicles, the leading coach being in maroon livery. The original station at Fleet, known for a while as 'Fleet Pond' after a local landmark, was built in 1847 and located on the west side of the road bridge, but when the line was quadrupled in 1904 new station premises were built on the east side of the road. *Ian Wright*

The line between Woking and Basingstoke is straight for much of its length and the gradients, such as they are, are almost imperceptible, so it presents a challenge to railway photographers. One of the most rewarding locations is this spot in the deep cutting between Hook and Winchfield where a road crosses the railway tracks on a very high and quite impressive bridge, providing a nicely balanced location. In this illustration Bulleid 'West Country' Class No.34021 *Dartmoor* whisks a Bournemouth to Waterloo express along the level section at the approach to Winchfield station on 6th July 1962. *John Beckett*

The 'Schools' Class locomotives were long associated with the South Eastern Section and only started to appear on the 'South Western' after their duties on the Charing Cross to Hastings line were taken over by diesel multiple units. In this picture No.30921 *Shrewsbury* is depicted approaching Basingstoke with an afternoon train from Waterloo on 1st September 1962. This particular locomotive spent many years at Dover and Ramsgate sheds while its final depot on the 'South Eastern' was Stewarts Lane. It was moved to Nine Elms shed in about July 1961 but was destined to spend only a relatively brief period working on the South Western Division, being withdrawn together with all other remaining 'Schools' Class engines at the end of 1962. *Shrewsbury* had a special claim to fame because in November 1961 it was fitted with an eight-wheeled tender from withdrawn 'Lord Nelson' Class 4-6-0 No.30854 *Howard of Effingham*. The four tracks in the background are known as Barton Mill sidings and are used to stable rolling stock of services that terminate at Basingstoke. *John Beckett*

A really fascinating study of a member of a small class of locomotives that became extinct as long ago as July 1957. This illustration shows 'Remembrance' Class 4-6-0 No.32329 *Stephenson* at Basingstoke on 22nd April 1956, just four months prior to its withdrawal. This picture gives an insight into the railway system in the Basingstoke area at that time – note the ancient van in the dock, the lower quadrant signals and Bulleid coach in carmine and cream livery which was in vogue at the time. No.32329 was one of seven L Class 4-6-4Ts built at Brighton works to the design of Lawson Billinton between 1914 and 1922 for working express passenger trains on the London to Brighton and Eastbourne services. The wheel arrangement was highly unusual and not used by any other railway company south of the river Thames. When the aforementioned routes were electrified in the 1930s all of the locomotives became redundant and Maunsell decided to rebuild them as 4-6-0 tender engines; all were converted between 1934 and 1936, being known as N15X Class. During the Second World War some members of the class worked on the Great Western Railway but during the BR years they were allocated to Basingstoke shed for secondary duties. Withdrawals commenced in February 1955 when No.32328 *Hackworth* was taken out of service and the last survivor of this little-photographed class was No.32331 *Beattie* which survived until July 1957. What an absolute gem of a photograph! *R.C. Riley*

The 9F Class 2-10-0s were versatile and powerful and are widely regarded as one of the most successful, if not *the* most successful, of the BR Standard designs. They were introduced in 1954 for working heavy mineral trains and a total of 251 engines was constructed, mostly at Crewe works, but a number were built at Swindon, including No.92220 *Evening Star* which was the last steam locomotive constructed by British Railways. Large numbers of the class were based at New England (Peterborough) and Doncaster sheds on the East Coast main line, and Wellingborough for working coal trains along the Midland main line; in addition there was a substantial allocation at Western Region depots in south Wales and a handful were based on the SR in the early 1960s for working oil trains from Fawley. The 9Fs will probably best be remembered, however, for their tremendous feats of haulage on two fiercely graded routes, the Tyne Dock to Consett line, where they powered very heavy trains of iron ore, and the legendary Somerset & Dorset route (S&D) where, on one occasion, *Evening Star* took a twelve coach train weighing 426 tons unassisted over the line's daunting 1 in 50 inclines. What better tribute to the 9Fs' capabilities could there be? In this picture No.92001 is depicted pulling out of Basingstoke on a train to Manchester in August 1965; it was based at Tyseley at the time of this picture so presumably worked as far as Birmingham. This locomotive was one of the small number of 9Fs that were used on the S&D in the early 1960s, but it is unlikely to be unduly exerted on this run compared to past exploits between Bath and Bournemouth! *Ian Wright*

A picture of N15X Class 4-6-0 No.32329 *Stephenson* appears elsewhere in this album but the author could not resist including a further shot of this rarely photographed class, which was taken at Andover Junction on 8th July 1956 when it was working the RCTS 'Wessex Wyvern' rail tour. It was withdrawn from traffic during the following month. It certainly does not look like an engine fit only for scrap! *R.C. Riley*

A tall bracket signal neatly frames Bulleid 'West Country' Pacific No.34100 *Appledore* as it pulls out of Andover Junction station with an unidentified London-bound train on 6th September 1964. That date was of particular significance for travellers on the Waterloo to West of England line because it was the very last day of steam operation prior to the introduction on the following day of a revised Waterloo to Exeter service worked by WR diesels. The 'Southern' route to the south-west had long been famous because many trains conveyed through coaches to resorts on the Devon/Cornwall coast and it was thought at the time that the withdrawal of this facility coupled with the longer journey times, not to mention the withdrawal of the 'Atlantic Coast Express', was the beginning of the end for the line. *Roy Denison*

Photographed on a very gloomy 24th February 1963, Bulleid Pacific No.34062 *17 Squadron* passes Grateley with a morning Salisbury to Basingstoke semi-fast service. In times gone by Grateley was the junction for the branch to Amesbury and Bulford, a service that was withdrawn from 30th June 1952. Note the pockets of lying snow which serve as reminders that Great Britain had just endured one of the worst winters in living memory. The date of this photograph may well be particularly remembered by many readers because that was the day that the legendary Gresley Pacific No.60022 *Mallard* worked an enthusiasts' special down the Waterloo to West of England line. *John Beckett*

Opposite: The Bulleid Light Pacifics had distinctive nameplates usually accompanied by a crest or shield and in this picture the nameplate of 'Battle of Britain' Class No.34050 *Royal Observer Corps* and the regimental crest are prominent. A member of the Royal Observer Corps is entitled to a long service medal after twelve years service and, accordingly, when No.34050 had been in traffic that length of time it was decided to decorate the locomotive with the appropriate plaques. This was done during a ceremony at Waterloo station on 2nd July 1961, after which the engine worked a special train to Bournemouth conveying members of the corps. This picture was taken at Andover Junction on 6th September 1964. *Roy Denison*

Surrounded by allotments, chalk downland and located in a deep cutting, Salisbury Tunnel Junction and its adjacent tunnel (over which the photographer is standing) are distinctive landmarks on the Waterloo to West of England line. Part of the junction is seen here with an unknown BR Standard Class 4MT 4-6-0 taking the line towards Southampton with what was presumably a train from either Cardiff or Bristol to Portsmouth. The tracks on the left lead to London. The signal box that controlled movements at this important junction is in the middle of the picture and it is one that was doubtless very eerie at night-time due to its location and not at all suitable for any signalman of a nervous disposition. One wonders whether one of the signalmen based here lived in the adjacent cottage and was occasionally tempted to nip home for lunch between trains! This picture was taken on 17th July 1964. *Colour-Rail*

(10/50)
12M.

SOUTHERN
BRITISH RAILWAYS
REGION

(787)

FROM WATERLOO TO

SALISBURY

Salisbury has always been something of a railway crossroads where trains on the Waterloo to West of England line met those on the cross country Portsmouth to Bristol and Cardiff route. The same is true today but Salisbury station and its environs have changed markedly since this photograph was taken, looking westwards, in mid-1966. Salisbury was once served by two stations, one 'Southern' and another Great Western, used by trains on the Westbury and Bristol route, and the layout and infrastructure seen here reflect this to some degree, even more than thirty years after the GWR station's demise on 12th September 1932. The former GWR tracks are those on the right of the shot: note the Great Western style signal box and lower quadrant signals. The rest of the scene presents a veritable forest of signals, telegraph poles, lighting standards and water cranes and, in the middle of the picture, another signal box. Rather strangely, when this picture was taken there was no sign of 'life' whatsoever and no trains or locomotives are visible, not even on the locomotive shed which can just be discerned in the far distance. Perhaps the shot was taken early on a Sunday morning! The main Salisbury shed dated from 1901 and boasted ten roads, and was an important depot because of the practice of changing engines at Salisbury. In later years at the end of steam on the SR withdrawn locomotives were congregated there prior to being towed away for scrapping in south Wales and mourning enthusiasts were no doubt frequent visitors. *Stuart Ackley collection*

An unidentified westbound train waits to leave Salisbury behind 'West Country' Class Pacific No.34036 *Westward Ho* on 17th March 1964. The train is signalled to take the Exeter line but, somewhat unusually, No.34036 is hauling an assortment of GWR and LMSR stock, so this is something of a mystery working. Apart from the abolition of semaphore signalling at Salisbury which has already been mentioned, other changes have included the downgrading of the platform on the left of the picture, which is no longer in regular use, and the construction of a diesel depot roughly on the site of the former GWR station premises on the extreme left of the shot. Only one branch line radiated from Salisbury, the route to Wimborne which served a thinly populated area and had a very sparse service; this was withdrawn on 4th May 1964. *Stuart Ackley collection*

An up stopping train, headed by Bulleid 'Battle of Britain' Pacific No.34086 *219 Squadron* leaves Buckhorn Weston tunnel, between Templecombe and Gillingham, on 3rd August 1964. The village of Buckhorn Weston, from which the tunnel takes its name, is located about a mile from the western end of the tunnel, on the northern side of the line. There is a dip after Templecombe as the line loses height before it crosses the river Cale, a tributary of the river Stour, but after that point it climbs into the tunnel, mostly at 1 in 100, the top of the climb being reached at the eastern portal. Note the change of gradient which is clearly visible in this photograph. The train seen here had already started the descent to Gillingham, also at 1 in 100. *John Beckett*

SALISBURY TO YEOVIL

In marked contrast to its filthy condition in a previous picture, Bulleid 'West Country' Pacific No.34108 *Wincanton,* in quite presentable external order, coasts into Templecombe with an unidentified down local train on 28th June 1964. This station is famous because it was the junction for the cross-country route from Bath to Bournemouth, the legendary Somerset & Dorset line, which passed underneath the LSWR main line just in front of the water tank that can be seen on the left. Templecombe station is located on a gradient of 1 in 80 against westbound trains and this is clearly visible in the picture, but such gradients are most unlikely to have unduly bothered *Wincanton*'s crew who had only a three-coach load behind them. The use of such a large and powerful locomotive, which weighed almost as much as the load it was pulling, seems to be very wasteful and it is no wonder that the WR (who had taken over the line in a boundary change) were anxious to rationalise the service on the route which must have been very expensive to operate. *Roy Denison*

In the days of steam the more glamorous express passenger locomotives always seemed to catch the eye of railway photographers and consequently more 'run of the mill' engines were often overlooked. Bulleid's Q1 0-6-0s were frequently shunned by photographers because that were regarded as unphotogenic, and the fact that they were very reliable and powerful performers seemed to count for nothing. During the compilation of this album dozens of pictures of Bulleid Pacifics were submitted but it soon became clear that shots of Maunsell's S15s would be in short supply – presumably photographers did not find them sufficiently attractive. In this rare view of one of these locomotives at work No.30831 is seen simmering in platform one at Templecombe with (what appears to be) a Salisbury to Exeter local train some time in the early 1960s. Despite serving only a small rural community the Southern Railway rebuilt the premises in 'Art Deco' style in the late 1930s and created quite a commodious station with three platforms and a refreshment room. Trains on the Somerset & Dorset line (S&D) used platform three which is hidden from view behind the signal box. When the S&D line closed in 1966 Templecombe station was shut at the same time and subsequently demolished but, following years of campaigning by local groups, it reopened on a trial basis in 1983. The reopening of the station has been a major success and it is now served by many trains on the Waterloo to Exeter line – what a pity the original premises were knocked down by BR. *Roy Denison*

Maunsell 'Mogul' No.31632, powering the 11.12am Exeter Central to Salisbury train, climbs the 1 in 80 gradient between Sherborne and Milborne Port on 18th May 1964. The train's formation consists of two 3-sets, the leading set being of Bulleid design while the set on the rear is made up of BR Standard coaches. Built at Ashford works in March 1931 this machine lasted in service until September 1964. At one time during its career No.31632 was based at Dorchester shed but spent its last years in traffic at Yeovil. *Colour-Rail*

The West of England to Waterloo line as many people will remember it! Bulleid 'Merchant Navy' Class No.35012 *United States Lines* powers along near Bradford Abbas, east of Yeovil, with an unidentified London-bound working in May 1964. A few weeks after this scene was recorded No.35012 was used on the RCTS 'Solway Ranger' rail tour from Leeds to Carlisle via Carnforth and back to Leeds via the Settle & Carlisle line. The train also visited some secondary routes in the Carlisle and Workington areas. On the return journey from Carlisle the Pacific ran like an engine possessed with the 17.45 miles from Appleby to Ais Gill summit, which is mostly on a gradient of 1 in 100, being covered in 17min. 41sec. – a truly epic performance. The load was nine coaches, totalling about 300 tons gross weight. *Roy Hobbs*

The 11.12am from Exeter is seen again, this time just after leaving Yeovil Junction on 26th March 1964, but on this occasion it was apparently extended to Waterloo. The train engine is Bulleid 'Battle of Britain' Pacific No.34080 *74 Squadron* while the pilot locomotive is BR Standard Class 4MT No.75000. This was a most unusual combination (not so rare in times gone by on the nearby Somerset & Dorset line!) and it must be assumed that something was amiss with the Pacific and the pilot engine, which was based at Yeovil at the time of this photograph, was provided as a precaution. It will be noted, however, that when the train passed the photographer's vantage point both locomotives seemed to be working very hard indeed on the rising gradient towards Sherborne. What a memorable sight and sound! Note the signal on the extreme right of the photograph – presumably it was placed there so it could be easily 'sighted' by footplatemen. *Gerald Daniels*

An engine change at Yeovil Junction. BR Standard Class 5MT No.73112 *Morgan le Fay* has just been removed from a down train, which is out of sight in the platform, while 'Battle of Britain' Pacific No.34061 *73 Squadron* 'blows off' impatiently as it waits to take over for the rest of the run, presumably through to Exeter Central. No.34061 was not destined to last much longer in service and was withdrawn from traffic in August 1964. This picture is thought to have been taken in May 1964. The original station layout at Yeovil Junction was inadequate and between 1907 and 1909 the premises were rebuilt to provide two fast tracks through the station with two slow lines to serve the platform faces, as seen here. In addition there was a down loop on which No.73112 is standing in this picture and also an up loop from where 'pull-push' services to Yeovil Town started. In later years the down platform was taken out of use and all services concentrated on the former up island platform. The scale of the rationalisation here was so severe that, incredibly, for a time it was not possible to pass trains in the station but this regrettable situation was later rectified.
Gerald Daniels

In the early 1920s the Southern Railway's Traffic Manager was keen to have locomotives capable of handling a 500-ton train at an average speed of 55mph and in August 1926 his prayers were answered when the first 'Lord Nelson' Class locomotive emerged from Eastleigh works. It was hailed as the most powerful express locomotive in the country and, after months of trials and evaluation, the first batch of ten locomotives started to enter traffic from May 1928 onwards, whilst a further five were built in late 1929, giving a total of sixteen members of the class. Despite the extensive design work and test running of the prototype the class generally failed to live up to expectations in everyday service: the fact that there were only sixteen examples meant that drivers did not handle the engines on a regular basis and this may have been part of the cause. Drivers often preferred the smaller 'King Arthur' Class locomotives, especially west of Salisbury. In 1939, however, the fortunes of the 'Lord Nelson' Class changed for the better when Bulleid, who had succeeded Maunsell, fitted them with Lemaitre multiple-jet exhausts plus a large diameter chimney and the engines were transformed overnight. Later, modifications were made to the cylinders which brought about further improvements in their performance and all of the unfulfilled promises of the earlier years were forgotten. In this undated shot No.30862 *Lord Collingwood* is seen easing away from Basingstoke with (what appears to be) a Waterloo to Bournemouth train. This particular engine was one of the final batch to be built, in October 1929, and survived to be one of the last two locomotives in traffic, being withdrawn in October 1962.
Ken Wightman / David Clark collection

A total of thirty 700 Class locomotives was built in 1897 to the design of Dugald Drummond by Dubs & Co. in Glasgow for goods work on the London & South Western Railway. These locomotives closely resembled Drummond's similar designs for companies north of the border. The 700s weighed a total of 86 tons 6 cwt but had 23,540lb tractive effort and when they were built the class had identical boilers to those used on the M7 Class 0-4-4Ts. Urie rebuilt the whole class with superheaters between 1921 and 1929 and the boiler pressure and cylinder diameter were also increased. In addition, the smokeboxes were extended and the frames lengthened at the front end to accommodate this alteration. The first withdrawals were made in 1957 but many of the class remained in traffic until 1962, the final survivors being taken out of service at the end of that year. The example seen here posing on Basingstoke shed on an unknown date is nicely cleaned No.30368 which was one of the last survivors. Note the distinctive diamond-shaped Dubs & Co. brass works plate on the centre splasher. *Derek Penney*

BRITISH RAILWAYS
SOUTHERN REGION
Stock
787
(1/48) 12M
TO
BASINGSTOKE

The romance and glamour of the steam age were probably not wholly appreciated by the gentleman seen here as he shovels powdery ash out of the smokebox of 'King Arthur' Class 4-6-0 No.30777 *Sir Lamiel* at Basingstoke shed on 11th March 1961. Much of the work necessary to keep steam locomotives on the road was really arduous, dirty, often downright dangerous and none too well paid but, even so, many railwaymen seemed to relish the challenge of working with steam traction and took immense pride in the job, even if it involved getting up at 3.00am on a freezing January morning. Today enthusiasts would doubtless queue up for the privilege of being able to empty *Sir Lamiel*'s smokebox. How times have changed! *John Beckett*

A stranger on the 'Southern'? At the time of this photograph in August 1964 BR Standard Class 4MT No.75016 was officially allocated to Nuneaton shed on the London Midland Region so its appearance on a westbound goods train west of Basingstoke, on the face of it, was quite remarkable. No.75016, however, is recorded as having arrived at Eastleigh works for repair between 4th May and 6th June 1964 so it is very likely that it was 'running in' after a general repair there, or perhaps it had been commandeered for a time by the SR operating authorities following its release from works because of a motive power shortage – a not unknown occurrence. One wonders when it returned 'home' to Nuneaton. *Derek Penney*

BASINGSTOKE TO SOUTHAMPTON

Another westbound goods train photographed west of Basingstoke, but this time with 'ordinary' SR motive power. Here, Maunsell U Class No.31801 plods along the down slow line with a heavy goods in the autumn of 1963, its headcode denoting a train bound for Southampton Docks. No.31801 was originally built as a South Eastern & Chatham Railway K Class 2-6-4T; all of the locomotives were named after rivers and were thus known as the 'River' Class. No.31801 was formerly named *River Darenth*. In August 1927 one of the K Class locomotives was derailed at high speed near Sevenoaks and it was decided to rebuild all of the 2-6-4Ts as 2-6-0 tender engines. The rebuilt engines were known as the U Class and they were used principally on intermediate passenger duties, such as semi-fast and cross-country workings. Some members of the class were, however, built new to the design of the converted engines, but with some detail differences. Withdrawals commenced in late 1962 with the bulk of the class being taken out of service in 1963/64, although a few locomotives managed to survive into 1966 on ballast duties in connection with the Bournemouth Line electrification, mainly working from Guildford shed. No.31801 lasted until June 1964. *Derek Penney*

'Lord Nelsons' in the shadows. No.30861 *Lord Anson* passes Worting Junction with the Southern Counties Touring Society's 'South Western Limited' rail tour on 2nd September 1962. The locomotive worked the train through from Waterloo to Exeter and later powered the return train as far as Salisbury, from where the participants returned to London via Eastleigh using other motive power. It is understood that this was the last 'Lord Nelson' working to Exeter. By the time of this photograph the 'Lord Nelsons' were being rapidly phased out with two being withdrawn in August, two more in September and the last two survivors, Nos.30861 and 30862 *Lord Collingwood* in October. The train seen here was not *Lord Anson*'s swan song on passenger work however, because on 8th September it appeared on the non-stop 10.00am Bournemouth Central to Waterloo and the 5.30pm back to Bournemouth West. Note the varying positions of the roof boards on the Bulleid and BR Standard coaches forming the train. *Derek Penney*

A number of BR Standard Class 4MT 2-6-0s were based on the SR, most being allocated to Eastleigh while Bournemouth, Salisbury and Redhill depots also had a handful. The class was constructed over a fairly long period, the first locomotive appearing from the former Horwich works (near Bolton) in December 1952 while the last engine to be built was out-shopped by Doncaster works in October 1957. The Class 4MT 2-6-0s were designed for local passenger and cross-country work and in the early 1960s could be found on five regions, the exception being the Western Region. The London Midland, Southern and Scottish regions each had around thirty locomotives allocated. A total of 115 engines was eventually constructed. The example seen here, No.76067, was photographed at Worting Junction on 14th May 1966 while powering what seems to be a passenger train bound for the Southampton line. This particular locomotive, which spent all of its brief working life on the SR based at either Eastleigh or Salisbury sheds, was one of a batch built at Doncaster and No.76067 was released for service in August 1956, lasting until the end of steam traction on the SR in July 1967. Note that it was fitted with one of the large, high-sided 4,725 gallon tenders. *Martin Smith*

Worting Junction is, of course, the location at which the Bournemouth line diverges from the route to Salisbury and Exeter, and this picture gives an idea of the layout at this point. The track in the right foreground is the down Bournemouth line, while the adjacent track, on which Bulleid Pacific No.34023 *Blackmore Vale* is travelling, is the down Exeter line. The next track is used by up trains from Exeter, while the track atop the embankment is the up Bournemouth line which crosses the two Exeter lines on a girder bridge, known as Battledown flyover, this being out of the picture to the left. It should be pointed out that the physical connection between the routes is about half a mile or so east of this spot. The flyover and quadruple section of track at this point date from 30th May 1897. This portrait was taken in August 1962. *Alan Reeve*

The icy wastes of Hampshire – one can almost feel the unbearable cold in this photograph. The very severe winter of 1962/63 was one of the worst in living memory, when the temperature hardly rose above freezing point for weeks on end. In this picture a down express from Waterloo to the West of England, headed by Bulleid 'West Country' Pacific No.34026 *Yes Tor,* approaches the Battledown flyover on 5th January 1963. The Pacific is emitting a splendid trail of smoke that no doubt pleased the photographer. One wonders how he was able to take such an evocative picture in the numbing cold – perhaps it was a case of keeping his hands in his pockets until the very last moment and simply hoping that the camera had not succumbed to the Siberian winter conditions. Full marks for a superb image and enduring the bitter weather. What a hero! *Alan Reeve*

Hampshire at almost the height of summer. Photographed in vastly different weather conditions to those seen in the previous illustration, Urie S15 Class 4-6-0 No.30514 is approaching Battledown flyover and heads in the direction of Salisbury with a short local passenger train in August 1962. The formation comprises a BR Standard 3-set supplemented by a Maunsell open second carriage dating from about 1933. Unlike sister engine No.30833, seen in a previous picture, which was built in the later Maunsell period, No.30514 was one of the earlier batch of S15 Class locomotives and this particular engine emerged from Eastleigh works in March 1921. They could be easily distinguished from the later locomotives because they had the running board raised over the cylinders and also had a different style of cab. Most of the class were based at Feltham shed for hauling express goods workings, while Salisbury also had a sizeable allocation; a small number were shedded at Redhill on the Central Section. The Urie-designed engines were the first to go, No.30514 lasting until July 1963. *Alan Reeve*

The overwhelming majority of Bournemouth line pictures submitted for this album feature Bulleid Pacifics, and for some reason not immediately apparent to the author, few people bothered to photograph the BR Standard Class 5MTs. This is a great pity because members of this class played a substantial part in the operation of the South Western Division right up to the end of steam traction. In this shot No.73029 is depicted approaching Micheldever with a down express on a sunny 23rd July 1966. This locomotive lasted until the curtain came down on steam traction on the SR on 9th July 1967 and during the final week it was very active, working the 4.51pm Basingstoke to Salisbury train followed by the 6.38pm Salisbury to Waterloo on 7th July. On the very last day of steam it powered the 9.47am Fratton to Clapham Junction empty coaching stock working. The location of Micheldever is well known to railway enthusiasts because at the time of this photograph and, for some years afterwards, a bank of sidings there was used as a dump for condemned rolling stock *en route* to the scrap yard; the front ends of one or two withdrawn electric units can just be discerned on the extreme right of the shot. *Roy Denison*

Between Basingstoke and Winchester the Bournemouth line passes through a very thinly populated area and Micheldever is the only station on the 18 miles-long stretch between those points. Here, a 'Merchant Navy' Pacific No.35027 *Port Line,* bereft of its front number plate, coasts downhill through the station with a down express on the same day that the previous picture was taken. The line descends from Litchfield tunnel, about

two miles north of here, on a gradient of generally 1 in 252 virtually all of the way to Southampton so firemen of southbound trains were not unduly strained on this stretch. Micheldever station was, unbelievably perhaps, originally opened as 'Andover Road' simply because it was, at that time, the nearest station to Andover! It was renamed in February 1856. The station building at Micheldever is really attractive, being constructed of local flint with yellow brick quoins (cornerstones) and, in addition, the building has an all-round verandah which gives it additional appeal. Around the turn of the century an island platform was built at Micheldever following quadrupling of the tracks through the station, but this later fell into disuse as fast trains sped through without stopping, and the slow trains used the original separate up and down platforms which were served by the loop lines. In 1966, however, the loop lines were removed and the island platform came into its own once again. The signal box, which is just visible above the third and fourth coaches of the train, lasted until 13th November 1966. *Roy Denison*

'A thorn among roses' might well have been the comment of 'Southern' enthusiasts when they saw a Western Region pannier tank locomotive on Eastleigh shed. Towards the end of steam traction on BR Eastleigh works became responsible for the repair of several hitherto unaccustomed locomotive classes including, for a time, Ivatt Class 4MT 2-6-0s and Stanier Class 8F 2-8-0s. On one occasion in 1965 an ex-works 8F famously powered a Waterloo to Basingstoke rush-hour commuter train! Here, pannier tank engine No.9764 poses on Eastleigh shed on 2nd September 1962 accompanied by representatives of two of Maunsell's less numerous classes, W Class 2-6-4T No.31916 and Q Class 0-6-0 No.30530. It is likely that, at the time of this photograph, only pannier tank locomotives actually allocated to the SR were being overhauled at Eastleigh because No.9764 was based at Yeovil Town shed, which came under SR jurisdiction, while two other examples, Nos.4698 and 9770, that were at the works for repair at the same time were based at Nine Elms. Note that No.9764 is proudly displaying a 71H shed allocation plate, this being the code given to the former GWR shed at Yeovil, which had been known as 82E under the WR, when it came under SR control in the mid-1950s. This shed was closed on 5th January 1959 and No.9764 was re-allocated, but the staff at Yeovil Town shed were clearly in no hurry to fix a 72C plate. *Derek Penney*

A down express from Waterloo passes Millbrook station, in the Southampton suburbs, behind Bulleid 'West Country' Pacific No.34036 *Westward Ho* in April 1965. The track layout between Southampton Central and Millbrook was altered radically in 1934/35 when the former station was rebuilt and the number of through tracks increased from two to four, with the quadrupled track section being extended to beyond Millbrook station to increase operational flexibility. A new station building, located in the middle of the four-track through-line section, was provided at Millbrook in 1935 and also a new signal box to the west of the station premises. The two tracks seen here on the right lead to the Western docks. The goods yard at Millbrook was closed in July 1967 and, at the time of writing, the site is occupied by a freightliner terminal. Regrettably, many of the buildings seen in the background of this picture were later demolished to make way for a road improvement scheme. *Ian Wright*

SOUTHAMPTON TO WEYMOUTH

The railway enthusiast fraternity must have been amazed by the decision of the SR hierarchy to run their official 'farewell to steam' trains on 2nd July 1967, which was a week before steam was actually due to finish, so this alone ensured that these trains would hardly rank as a significant landmark in the history of SR steam traction! Provisional plans apparently envisaged no fewer than five specials, but reality prevailed and this number was whittled down to two, one from Waterloo to Weymouth while the other train operated from Waterloo to Bournemouth. The first special left London at 9.55am to Weymouth with 'Merchant Navy' Class No.35008 *Orient Line* in charge and it has to be said that, for a locomotive facing oblivion a week later, it gave a good account of itself, reaching a top speed of 88mph on the down journey and 90mph on the return run. An added bonus for those who patronised the Weymouth train was the use of sister engine No.35007 *Aberdeen Commonwealth* as far as Bournemouth, a rare pairing of two 'Merchant Navy' Pacifics. The other train departed from Waterloo at 12.20pm, ten minutes ahead of the 'Bournemouth Belle', with No.35028 *Clan Line* in charge and this train made the customary water stop at Southampton. The fare demanded to travel on the Bournemouth train was £4, an outrageously high fare for that time, and many enthusiasts must have felt cheated when they could have travelled on the 9.33am excursion to Bournemouth behind No.34025 *Whimple* at a fraction of the cost. In this portrait *Clan Line* is seen near Beaulieu Road with the returning special from Bournemouth. Note that the formation includes a Gresley buffet car. *Derek Penney*

A very unusual piece of equipment at Brockenhurst is this luggage platform which makes life much easier for the station staff. The platform is interlocked with the signalling system and carries a red lamp on top of the pole. This picture was taken on 26th March 1966. *Stuart Ackley collection*

The last steam-worked passenger branch in Great Britain was the Brockenhurst to Lymington line which opened as far as Lymington Town on 12th July 1858 and was extended to Lymington Pier station, where ferry connections are made to the Isle of Wight, on 1st May 1884. Towards the end of steam traction on the SR this hitherto quiet backwater achieved a high profile and many enthusiasts made the pilgrimage to sample the delights of steam haulage along a branch line, an experience that, by that time, could not be found on any other BR line in Great Britain. In this picture BR Standard Class 4MT 2-6-4T No.80146 awaits departure from Brockenhurst shortly before steam was ousted by diesel units on 3rd April 1967. The attractive little headboard says it all! *Ian Foot*

Another scene taken at Brockenhurst, this time showing Maunsell Q Class 0-6-0 No.30548 waiting in a siding before shunting the stock of the 4.07pm to Bournemouth West via Ringwood into the station on 6th July 1961. The rake of coaches forming the train consists of Bulleid 3-set 825 and two Maunsell vehicles, quite a long formation for a train on the Ringwood line – perhaps this working was specially strengthened to cater for schoolchildren. The photographer states that two or three schoolgirls, who were in high spirits apparently after completing their GCE examinations, contrived to miss the train and would probably have had to wait for an hour. One wonders how their parents would have reacted to such silly behaviour! During his sojourn at Brockenhurst station the photographer noted no fewer than six locomotives in twenty minutes, including 'Merchant Navy' Pacific No.35005 *Canadian Pacific* on the 1.30pm Waterloo to Weymouth train. *John Langford*

A scene at Lymington Junction, a location that has altered a great deal since this shot was taken in July 1962; in this view M7 Class 0-4-4T No.30053, in very respectable external condition, has just come off the Lymington branch and heads for Brockenhurst. The line diverging sharply to the right behind the train is the original 60½ miles-long route from Southampton to Dorchester via Wimborne which was promoted by Mr. A.L. Castleman, a Wimborne solicitor, and became known as 'Castleman's Corkscrew' due to its sinuous nature. At the time of its construction in the mid-1840s places like Ringwood and Wimborne were much more important than Bournemouth which was yet to develop as a premier seaside resort. The Wimborne line was reduced to little more than a rural byway when the direct route to Bournemouth opened and it eventually closed to passengers on 4th May 1964, the meagre service provided by BR no doubt hastening its demise. The line going almost straight ahead in the middle of the picture is the main line to Bournemouth while the Lymington branch curves away to the left. Lymington Junction signal box was closed in 1978 when a new signalling panel came into use at Brockenhurst, thus rendering many signal boxes in the area redundant. It should be noted that the junction at this spot was abolished some years ago and Lymington branch trains now operate from Brockenhurst along a separate single track that runs parallel to the Bournemouth main line before they turn off. *Alan Reeve*

One of the most interesting workings on the SR in the mid-1960s was the 10.08am York (8.30am from Newcastle in the summer) to Poole through train which regularly brought 'foreign' motive power onto the Region. This train was latterly booked for diesel haulage north of Banbury but was rostered for steam south thereof and at one time often produced Western Region 'Hall' Class engines. In the summer of 1966 Stanier Class 5MT 4-6-0s were staple motive power south of Banbury and in this view No.45493 is depicted working hard in charge of the southbound train on the short, sharp 1 in 103 climb away from Lymington Junction in September 1966. This locomotive became a regular sight on the south coast during that summer, together with sister engine No.44942 which was also a frequent performer. Sometimes when Banbury shed was really hard-pressed for engines quite extraordinary classes would be turned out for this train such as LMSR Class 8F No.48276 on 22nd February 1966, while BR Standard Class 9F No.92002 appeared on the northbound train on 20th August 1966, presumably after

previously working the southbound train. The Stanier Class 5MTs were booked to stable during the weekend at Bournemouth shed but the SR operating authorities (in reality steam fans in the Wimbledon diagramming office!) often used them on the 8.55am Sunday only Bournemouth to Waterloo and 8.30pm return. Thirty-five different 'Black Fives' were recorded in 1966, but sadly these workings ceased abruptly following the closure of the Great Central main line in early September and the South Western Division lost some of its variety of locomotive classes. *Ian Wright*

The reasonably clean cab-side and smokebox door, plus the homemade front number plate of Bulleid Pacific No.34102 *Lapford*, only serve to highlight the appalling condition of the locomotive as it stands in Pokesdown station. No.34102 was working the 11.07am Bournemouth Central to Waterloo on 21st September 1966, a train which was advertised to convey full dining facilities on Mondays to Fridays with a buffet car only on Saturdays. Unbelievably, *Lapford* soldiered on until the very last week of steam in July 1967 so, perhaps, its mechanical state was much better than its external appearance in this picture would suggest. Its final recorded passenger run was on the 6.49am Salisbury to Waterloo on 5th July 1967. *Martin Smith*

The western end of Bournemouth Central station is seen in this photograph which was taken from a down train awaiting departure in September 1965. This shot shows the old track layout and mechanical signalling arrangements prior to the considerable changes made in connection with electrification. There is not a third rail in sight! The lady and gentleman walking purposefully along the up platform with their suitcases appear to have walked down from the shed, but perhaps it is more likely that they had been waiting to join an up train that had come to a stand further up the platform than they had anticipated. Note the station's very long down platform which is no doubt invaluable operationally at times of heavy traffic and also was a great advantage to train spotters who were able to see exactly what was happening on the shed. The platform was lengthened in 1928 so that it could accommodate two twelve-coach trains. Note the prominent green-painted running-in board. In the very earliest days of railways in the area the small hamlet of Bournemouth was accessed by a horse-drawn carriage from Hamworthy, but this situation improved for the better in 1862 when Christchurch was reached by a branch from Ringwood; this line was extended to Bournemouth in 1870. The entire through route between Brockenhurst and Poole did not come into operation until 1888. The motive power depot is visible in the middle of the picture. The first shed on this site dated from the opening by the LSWR of Bournemouth station in 1885 but the four-road building seen here largely dates from the mid-1930s, when improvements were carried out by the Southern Railway. A new asbestos roof was added by BR after the Second World War. *Stuart Ackley collection*

BRITISH RAILWAYS   B 787/123

LUGGAGE

To

BOURNEMOUTH
CENTRAL

This magnificent panoramic view of the Dorset countryside is considerably enhanced by the presence of Bulleid 'Merchant Navy' Pacific No.35028 *Clan Line* as it takes a down stopping train across the heathland. This picture was taken on 29th April 1967 near Moreton. *John Beckett*

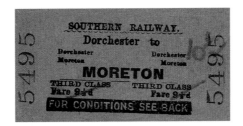

Bulleid 'West Country' Pacific No.34025 *Whimple* hauling the 8.30am Waterloo to Weymouth train is depicted near Moreton, also on 29th April 1967. At this point in the journey the formation would have consisted of only four or five carriages, because the main portion of the train, which probably conveyed a buffet car, would have been detached at Bournemouth. There is no doubt that passengers travelling from London to Weymouth enjoyed a wide variety of landscapes, from the chalk downland and New Forest in Hampshire to the distinctive heathland of Dorset. *John Beckett*

SOUTHAMPTON TO WEYMOUTH

If there was ever a competition to find the most unconventional railway station in Great Britain, Dorchester South would be a strong contender. Originally, the straight platform seen here formed the terminus of the line from Southampton via Ringwood and Wimborne, the famous 'Castleman's Corkscrew' route, and its energetic promoter cherished hopes of an extension to Exeter. The Great Western Railway (GWR) put paid to these aspirations when it opened its line to Weymouth in January 1857 and the LSWR laid a single track curve to connect with the GWR line. Trains serving Dorchester station were forced to reverse, but in May 1879 the connection was doubled and a curved down platform was commissioned but, most strangely, no corresponding up platform was provided and up services were still obliged to reverse into the original platform. In the late 1930s the Southern Railway had demolished the overall roof that had been provided over the up platform, but surprisingly nothing was done to eliminate the time-consuming reversal necessary for up trains. This crazy situation continued for a further ninety-one years until sanity at last prevailed in 1970, when a new curved up platform was brought into use by BR. In this picture BR Standard Class 5MT No.73002 waits in the former up platform with a local train to Bournemouth Central on 30th July 1966. *Les Dench*

One of the best spots in the south of England to witness steam locomotives really working hard uphill was Upwey bank, just outside Weymouth, where heavy trains were given rear-end assistance on the difficult 1 in 50 climb which had to be tackled from a standing start in Weymouth station. On a clear day observers had a wonderful grandstand from where to view trains as they laboured up the incline, very often at little more than walking pace. Two tunnels near the summit of the climb, Bincombe North and South, added to the interest and in this illustration two grimy locomotives, BR Standard Class 5MT No.73002 and Bulleid 'Merchant Navy' No.35013 *Blue Funnel,* are seen emerging from Bincombe South tunnel with an unidentified northbound working on 2nd July 1966. *Martin Smith*

An afternoon passenger train, hauled by Bulleid 'Battle of Britain' Class Pacific No.34077, *603 Squadron* ascends Upwey bank, on the climb out of Weymouth, on 13th September 1962. The train engine's exhaust is being blown down by the strong easterly wind, totally obscuring BR Standard Class 5MT No.73029 pushing mightily at the rear. The stiff climb and the glorious vista that can be seen from other locations further up the line made this particular section of route a firm favourite with photographers. Banking engines 'dropped off' at Bincombe tunnel signal box, about four miles from Weymouth, where there was a siding (actually a crossover with plenty of space to stable a locomotive) for assisting locomotives between the up and down running lines. After giving rear-end assistance a banker would reverse into the siding and await a clear 'road' back to Weymouth. *John Beckett*

Unfortunately, for reasons unknown to the author, few colour pictures of steam traction appear to have been taken at Weymouth station, perhaps because photographers were always attracted by the spectacle of steam locomotives working to their limit on Upwey bank. Pictures were taken at Weymouth shed, however, and in this shot taken on 17th July 1965 BR Standard 4-6-0 No.73020, nearest to the camera, is seen 'blowing off' furiously. An Ivatt-designed Class 2MT 2-6-2T, No.41298, is also prominent and it is likely that this locomotive was used to haul Channel Islands boat trains between the station and Weymouth Quay, which involved negotiating the well-known Weymouth Quay tramway. What a great way to start your holiday, being steam-hauled along the streets of Weymouth, but one wonders how many passengers appreciated how privileged they were! Weymouth shed was built by the GWR and at one time the 'Southern' had its own shed adjacent to Weymouth station, but this was closed in January 1939 when agreement was reached with the GWR regarding the use of their depot. *Alan Chandler*

A view of Weymouth shed believed to have been taken just a few weeks before steam traction bowed out – there does not seem to be much activity! The locomotives are (from l. to r.) BR Standard Class 4MT 2-6-4T No.80146 and Bulleid Pacific Nos.34018 *Axminster* and 34001 *Exeter*. The origins of this shed lie with the Great Western who constructed the main buildings in 1885. Originally, the shed had only a 49ft. 9in. turntable which was too small to turn some of the larger locomotives and in 1925 it was replaced by a turntable that was 65ft in diameter. Unlike other depots on the SR, this shed was relatively busy on the very last day of steam, 9th July 1967, because a boat-load of tomatoes from the Channel Islands required rapid onward movement due to the fact that they were 'perishable' goods. Three steam locomotives were provided to work the extra trains as far as Westbury and, in addition, Bulleid 'Merchant Navy' Class No.35030 *Elder Dempster Lines* was turned out to power an afternoon passenger train to Waterloo. *Colour-Rail*

Strictly speaking the West London Line from Clapham Junction to North Pole Junction is outside the geographical area of the southern counties, but for many years inter-regional trains routed this way generated a lot of interest among the railway enthusiast fraternity south of the river Thames, and at least all of the trains depicted here served the south coast and had SR motive power. This picture shows an unidentified southbound summer holiday train near Mitre Bridge Junction on 29th August 1959 with Bulleid Pacific No.34099 *Lynmouth* in charge. This machine was based at Brighton at the time of this photograph so it is reasonable to assume it was heading for either Brighton or Eastbourne. Note that *Lynmouth* has the original type of tender complete with the old style BR totem. The two discs on top of posts on the left hand side are banner repeater signals which are generally located in advance of signals that are less easily seen by enginemen due to obstructions such as bridges. *R. C. Riley*

The Billinton K Class 'Moguls' were nothing if not versatile and robust locomotives and, although they were really designed for goods traffic, on summer Saturdays they were often pressed into service on inter-regional trains, as seen here. The name on the side of the signal box immediately identifies the location of this picture, the train being the 11.24am Hastings to Leicester with No.32353 in command, and this shot was taken on 8th August 1959. This particular locomotive is in quite scruffy external condition, its dirty state possibly being explained by the fact that it was shedded at Three Bridges – sister locomotives based at Brighton were usually kept in much cleaner condition. *R.C. Riley*

Almost 'Southern' steam's last gasp. The 8th July 1967 was the penultimate day of steam traction on the SR and the Region's operating authorities had arranged for many of the remaining locomotives to be despatched to Salisbury and Weymouth sheds prior to disposal. This resulted in a mass migration of engines from the capital's last steam depot, Nine Elms, to Salisbury where a total of fifty-five locomotives were eventually gathered by the following evening. Some isolated steam workings did occur during the final weekend, however, and one of those concerned a special inter-regional train, the 11.26am from Portsmouth Harbour to Colne, which was powered by 'West Country' Pacific No.34037 *Clovelly*. This working is depicted passing through Kensington (Olympia) and it was presumably the very last scheduled steam-hauled passenger train to pass through the station – a moment in railway history. *Clovelly* had previously powered an overnight Waterloo to Portsmouth newspaper train and worked the Colne special after being turned at Fratton shed. It rounded off its very busy day by hauling the special 6.20pm Waterloo to Southampton Docks boat train which was the final steam departure from Waterloo in ordinary service.
Roy Denison